Small Conifers for Small Gardens

by

Robert L. Fincham

Coenosium Press
Eatonville WA

Small Conifers for Small Gardens

Dedication

This book is dedicated to the memory of the many people who shared their knowledge, plants, and friendship with me as I explored this fascinating world of dwarf and unusual conifers.

Above all, this book is dedicated to my best friend and wife, Dianne, who has been supportive throughout the many years that I have been consumed by my passion for conifers. Who carried much of the load when we were working to get the American Conifer Society organized and established. Who took pity on me when I started Coenosium Gardens and became a full working partner in the business. Last but not least, who brings a quality to my life which mere words cannot describe.

Acknowledgement

I would like to especially thank Edwin Smits, a Dutch conifer collector, nurseryman, and friend, whose assistance in the preparation of this book was invaluable. He spent many hours checking and verifying the information in this book to help make it the valuable resource I believe it to be.

Cover Photographs

The three cover photographs were taken at the garden of Kas Koemans, Boskoop, Holland. He passed away several years ago, but the new owner is still maintaining the beautifully landscaped grounds. Koemans specialized in collecting *Chamaecyparis* and *Cryptomeria* cultivars.

Frontispiece: *Chamaecyparis obtusa* 'Nana Lutea' at RHS Garden Wisely, Surrey, England

Text copyright © 2011 Robert L. Fincham

Photographs copyright © 2011 Robert L. Fincham

All rights reserved

Published in 2011 by
Coenosium Press
4412 354th Street East
Eatonville WA 98328

Printed by
Gorham Printing
3718 Mahoney Drive
Centralia WA 98531

ISBN 978-0-9837354-0-3

Table of Contents

Preface 6
Introduction 12
Small Conifer Landscapes 22
Abies 32
Cedrus 58
Chamaecyparis 76
Cryptomeria 108
Picea 116
Pinus 186
Pseudotsuga 254
Taxus 256
Thuja 262
Tsuga 264
Picture Credits 288
Index 289

Preface

The statement "A conifer is a cone bearing tree." is a very simplistic definition for a fascinating group of plants. Growing up in eastern Pennsylvania I came to know the eastern white pine (*Pinus strobus*) and the Canadian hemlock (*Tsuga canadensis*) quite well. I used to roam the woods of Carbon County and enjoy the scattered specimens of these two conifers along the streams and creeks of the lower areas between the ridges of the Appalacian Mountains. The scrubby pines of the ridge tops were not all that interesting, especially since animals (and swimming holes) were easier to find in the denser forests of the lowlands.

In the mid 1960's I attended Millersville State College (now Millersville University) and discovered horticulture when I took two semesters of basic botany. Only then did I realize the great diversity of conifers beyond the few species found where I grew up, but I did not pursue my new interest at that time.

I earned my degree in education and became a high school science teacher. While teaching, I met and married Dianne, who has come to understand my obsession with conifers. This obsession became apparent when we built our new home in 1974.

In 1972, when Dianne and I purchased an acre lot in the town of Lehighton, Pennsylvania, I immediately began to clear the weeds, sassafrass, and bitter cherries from the property. My first conifer plantings consisted of a double row of *Pinus strobus* for a windbreak. Then I visited several garden centers and chain stores looking for plants to landscape our new home. I planned to buy in the fall when stores were discounting unsold material. I was going to bury the pots for the winter and plant the following spring when the house was completed.

I did not want to have the same plants as everybody else in town so I tried to be selective. I avoided yews (*Taxus*) and Eastern Arborvitae (*Thjua occidentalis*) and chose junipers, spruces, and pines. I was assured that these were all dwarf plants that would not outgrow their spaces. It is hard to believe how naïve I was in those days. Out of thirty different plants, only two of them were still part of the landscape five years later.

As our home was being built, I discussed conifers with a teacher friend - Joe Lankalis. Joe has always been an exceptional naturalist with an almost photographic memory. He would intensely study a subject for a couple of years and then move on to something else. It just so happened that he was concentrating on dwarf conifers at this time and had become quite knowledgeable. He introduced me to a world I knew little about.

Joe and I visited a person in the area who had recently purchased a rare conifer nursery and was selling some of its material. I could hardly believe what I saw. Conifers that twisted or crawled on the ground and conifers that were very small or had fantastically colored foliage were scattered throughout the property. I traded a complete fern fossil I had collected in an old strip mine for several plants. These plants marked the start of my conifer collection that has become very extensive and quite well known.

We visited another fellow who lived outside of Philadelphia. Joe had purchased a number of plants from him for his own garden. Fred Bergman's gardens were like nothing I had even seen. I did not realize that conifers came in such a wide range of colors, shapes, and sizes. A nice mix of conifers and companion plants combined to create a garden that was not gaudy and had appeal all seasons of the year. Fred died a few years later, and his property was sold to a group of lawyers who auctioned the collection and built condos. I have always felt lucky to have seen that collection at its peak.

Joe and I then visited a man who lived several miles outside of Lehighton and who once had one of the largest conifer collections in the world. Layne Ziegenfuss and his Hillside Gardens Nursery were known throughout eastern North America as a source of rare conifers. He was very friendly and shared his knowledge and sources for rare and unusual conifers. Interestingly enough, his close friend, Greg Williams, was the former owner of the nursery Joe and I had visited earlier. Greg had recently moved to Vermont, and this had limited Layne's explorations for new conifers.

As Joe's interest in conifers waned, I developed a close friendship with Layne and learned even more about rare conifers and their origins. As my involvement became more intense, Layne put me in touch with a number of conifer people who made many positive influences on my life.

During the school year I was too busy to spend much time with my new hobby. However, during vacations I started making regular visits to many of these people and added to my collection. My trips into northern New Jersey and onto Long Island were made in a Nissan hatchback. I would leave home with a full tank of gas, no credit card or checkbook, and just the cash I felt I could spend. Many times I drove home with just enough money to pay the toll for the Delaware River Bridge.

Don and Hazel Smith owned Watnong Nursery in northern New Jersey, and by my third visit we had formed a friendship and would spend hours talking plants while enjoying lunch. Don specialized in *Chamaecyparis obtusa* and *Tsuga canadensis* and had an extensive collection. He even sold a large part of his inventory to me to help me start Coenosium Gardens.

Preface (cont.)

On Long Island were Joe Reis and Eddie Rezek who shared their enthusiasm and their plants with me on my many visits. Their neighborhoods were always easy to identify by the many special landscapes done with dwarf conifers.

Joe Burke showed me how to graft into the root crown of a conifer to produce a plant suitable for the bonsai enthusiast who does not want graft scar to show on his plant. Joe also lived on Long Island, and I spent many enjoyable hours with him discussing everything from conifers to sewing machines to WWII.

In the Hamptons was The Creeks, an estate owned by Alfonso Ossorio. Alfonso was an artist who used conifers as an art form and created a very special conifer landscape. Visits to Alfonso gave me many insights into using conifers in unique ways. When he died, his estate was made off limits to visitors, and I have not been able to see it mature.

I began Coenosium Gardens for several reasons. By 1979 I was an avid conifer collector. Whenever I lost a plant in my collection, I could not always replace it. Layne taught me how to graft to duplicate the plants in my collection. I decided to propagate extras and share them with other collectors. Coenosium Gardens was also an excellent way to make rare conifers available to anyone who wanted them. Many good conifers have been lost to cultivation because they were grown by people who did not share them.

Coenosium Gardens opened for business in 1979. Soon I was contacted by Gordon Bentham, a retired butcher from Victoria, British Columbia. Gordon wanted to trade rare conifers. He introduced himself with a package of six rare conifers and a long letter. We became good friends. Gordon shared conifers with people on the west coast of the United States as Layne Ziegenfuss and Greg Williams did on the east coast.

People all over the world have been collecting conifers since the early 1900's, but during the 1950's and 1960's there were few people in America doing any serious collecting. One of the biggest collections, William Gotelli's, had been donated to the National Arboretum and another, Colonel Robert H. Montgomery's, had been given to the New York Botanic Garden. Al Fordham, Head Propagator at the Arnold Arboretum, was building a substantial collection. A few wholesale nurseries were propagating some dwarf conifers, and a few collectors were scattered along the east coast. Everything was kept together by a number of enthusiastic people. Layne and Greg were busy collecting plants in various locations and sharing them with people who lived in other places. Don and Hazel Smith were running Watnong Nursery and educating the public by lecturing through the Northeast.

The late 1970's and early 1980's saw Coenosium Gardens become a major retail source of rare conifers. At about the same time a large wholesale nursery in Oregon began to dominate the rare conifer wholesale market. Jean Iseli was the driving force behind the whole concept of Iseli Nursery. It was Jean's dream to provide rare conifers to the wholesale market in specimen sizes. He forced other nurseries to diversify their offerings and to make a much wider selection of plant material available. Unfortunately, Jean died just as his plan was coming to fruition, and it has never reached its full potential as envisioned by him.

Whenever I visited the west coast, I always spent time with Jean looking at an amazing inventory of conifers and many other plants that were rare until he obtained them and increased their numbers. Jean and I shared ideas, dreams, and plants.

Not only have I traded many kinds of conifers with other collectors, but I have also given many plants to public gardens. I have always believed in educating the public about the kinds of conifers that are available and how to effectively use them in a garden. By giving plants to public institutions, I made certain that they were seen by people who may then want some of them for their own gardens. It was part of the same marketing technique used by Jean Iseli to create demand for his wholesale product.

I have seen conifers used in very special garden settings all over the world. The Gotelli Dwarf Conifer Collection in Washington, DC, was a regular destination for me when I lived in Pennsylvania. I enjoyed seeing the variety of conifers in mature sizes and quickly came to realize that not everyone defined dwarf in the same way.

On my first visit to England I was fortunate enough to be able to visit the Hillier Arboretum near Winchester. Sir Harold Hillier built a world famous nursery during the 1950's and 1960's from his family farm. Around his home he created a large arboretum featuring many of the Hillier introductions from all over the world. I saw many conifers at the arboretum that I had only ever read about. I often return there to see the changes as new plants are added and new plant beds are installed. Sir Harold donated the arboretum to the shire before his death, and it is maintained as a public arboretum.

Preface (cont.)

Near Windsor, England, is the British National Dwarf Conifer Collection, which was to be planted with only dwarf selections. I have photographed almost every plant in the collection several times over the years. Many excellent specimens may be seen in the gardens. John Bond started the plantings and soon found that many conifers labeled as dwarf, were anything but dwarf. A consistent program of bed rejuvenation and replanting prevents the beds from becoming overcrowded as the conifers grow. It is interesting to return every few years and observe the dwarf conifers as they mature.

Adrian Bloom showed me many ways to mix conifers with heather as he does in his gardens at Foggy Bottom. The color schemes are a virtual feast for the eyes. The larger conifers are planted to the rear while the dwarf conifers are mixed with heather toward the front of the beds. Together the conifers and heather provide color contrasts that vary with the seasons while the conifers provide a wide assortment of shapes and textures that are complemented by the wide spreading heathers.

I have traveled extensively in Holland, and to a lesser extent into Germany, Austria, Hungary, and the Czech Republic visiting gardens and studying conifer cultivars. Dick van Hoey Smith has been my host on many of these visits, and together we explored many old pinetums where I was able to see dwarf conifers that were over 100 years old. In Holland places like Arboretum Trompenburg, Pinetum Blijdenstein, Von Gimborn Pinetum, and Pinetum Dennenhorst were just a few of the more outstanding collections of mature conifers. Wiel Linssen has always shared his knowledge and his time whenever I visited his special garden of miniature conifers. His friend, Franz Esteldorfer, is just as sharing with his collection in Austria. Visits to the nurseries of the late Gunter Horstmann and the late Jan zu Jeddeloh in Germany were always very informative, and enjoyable as well. Jan Beran and Jaroslav Kazbal in the Czech Republic and Zsolt Mesterhazy in Hungary showed me many of the better conifer collections in their countries.

In 1986 Dianne and I moved to Oregon where I was to join Jean Iseli at Iseli Nursery. Jean was able to convince the Oregon Agriculture Department to allow me to bring 10,000 conifers into the state (6,000 of which were pines). Unfortunately I was never able to actually work with Jean because he died as we were packing to leave Pennsylvania. I spent only six months at Iseli nursery before Dianne and I decided to purchase Mitsch Nursery in Aurora, Oregon, which we operated for five years.

In 1992 I reentered teaching, and in 1996 Coenosium Gardens moved to Eatonville, Washington, where Dianne and I live today among almost four acres of conifer gardens. Teaching is my profession while Coenosium Gardens is a hobby/business that is almost another full time occupation.

The variety of conifers available today is much more extensive than anytime in the past. New selections are appearing on an almost daily basis. Some are improvements on older selections while others are not as good as some already available. Making suitable selections for the garden can be a very daunting task for the novice and even more so for the experienced gardener.

Throughout this book I will be sharing my experiences with and knowledge of conifers. A liberal use of photographs taken in gardens throughout the world will be used to show a mixture of conifers that are suitable for smaller gardens. Some will be easy to find, and others will be more difficult to obtain.

This book is not about the basics of landscape design. I do not even know the names of the many different schools of design. But I do know conifers, and I know how to use those conifers to create a satisfying and interesting landscape. Hopefully this book will provide new ideas about using smaller conifers in the landscape as well as provide information about which conifers are actually dwarf.

Read; learn; enjoy.

Introduction

Public gardens are usually very busy during the springtime. Visitors fill the walkways and wander the trails that go off to secluded areas of the gardens. The azaleas and rhododendrons are blooming. Later come the dogwoods and throughout the summer the perennials. People just love to see the flowers. When winter arrives, public gardens are usually deserted. When the flowers die, the visitors leave.

A plant flowers for a brief time. Either the plant has a short time to flower, such as an azalea, or it has a life span measured in one or two years. Even the perennials, some of which bloom much of the summer, are only pleasing for a few months out of the year.

Conifers are not as showy as the flowering plants, but they do produce flower-like structures, more correctly referred to as strobili, which provide spring color. More importantly, conifers can be enjoyed throughout the year for their foliage, which comes in a wide variety of colors, shapes, and textures.

Conifers provide the often unnoticed background for the colorful flower displays in public gardens throughout the spring and summer, providing a feeling of permanence not shared by their broad-leafed relatives. They also give a sense of a more temperate climate than do the broad-leafed plants with their bright flower displays that hint of the tropics.

The cone bearing trees, commonly called conifers, have existed since the days of the dinosaurs. They do not flower but reproduce through the formation of female and male reproductive organs that are held in separate places on the plant. Since these organs do not have flower parts, they are referred to as male and female strobili.

The pollen must go from the male strobilis to the female strobilis. Pollen is carried by the wind. Conifers produce copious amounts of pollen. Whenever I park my car near a grove of Douglas firs in the spring, it is rapidly covered with a thick layer of yellow dust. This dust is pollen. Spring finds the air full of pollen from conifers as it randomly drifts in search of female strobili.

When the pollen finds a female strobilis, fertilization occurs and a cone results. The cone is a woody structure that protects the seeds during their development. Every conifer has a different kind of cone, and the differences help considerably in their identification.

These female strobili are commonly called cones. These cones are ripening on a branch of a true fir. They were pollinated during the spring and mature through the summer. Each of the cone's scales protects a developing seed. In the fall these cones will disintegrate, and the winged seeds will fall to the ground. It is interesting to note that the female strobili of the true firs often develop near the top of the tree and the male strobili develop on the lower branches. This mechanism discourages self pollination as the pollen is seldom blown from the bottom to the top of a tree. The pollen will more likely come from a different plant.

A shaken branch full of ripe male strobili releases a cloud of pollen. Conifers are very prolific pollen producers, and during the spring many allergies are triggered by conifer pollen. In the Northwest, cars are coated with a yellow dust from all of the *Pseudotsuga menziesii* (Douglas fir) pollen that saturates the air during April and May.

Introduction (cont.)

Some conifers have a modified structure that is not an actual cone but rather a berry-like structure with an exposed seed. The yews are one of several groups of conifers that produce seed in this manner. The junipers also produce a berry-like structure but with the seed held inside.

The male strobili last a week or two before drying up and falling off the tree, but while present, they are often bright red and very visible to even the casual observer. The female strobili are often bright red as well, turning green and then brown after fertilization. Some true firs even produce very colorful blue female strobili.

While the reproductive organs are interesting, they are usually a minor reason for planting conifers in the landscape. The life span, foliage, and growth habit of the selected plant are the primary reasons for choosing a specific conifer. Foliage ranges from the fan-shaped foliage of the arborvitae and false cypress to the long, thin needles of the pines, the shorter needles of the spruce, and the flat needles of the firs.

Conifers may have common names that can vary from one area to another for the same plant. Names that are the same everywhere in the world regardless of the language spoken are the scientific names.

Basically, a common name is the name given to a plant growing in an area by the people who live in that area. It usually works just fine for those people. However, when an outsider visits or if the plant is mentioned outside of the local area, the name is often meaningless. One plant may have many common names, with no relationship between them. In America the red cedar often called the eastern red cedar is actually a juniper. The Atlantic white cedar is a *Chamaecyparis* while the white cedar is the eastern arborvitae and the western red cedar is the western arborvitae. All of these plants have fan-shaped sprays of foliage, which are nothing like those of the true cedars, which have clusters of thin, straight needles.

On a visit to a better garden center the homeowner will be barraged with scientific plant names that can be daunting to even the experienced landscaper. These names have meanings that are not necessarily all that difficult to sort out.

A scientific name is given to a plant to avoid any confusion with common names. A scientific name has two parts to it. The first part of the name is the genus of the plant while the second part of the name is the species. Instead of presenting a botany lesson, allow me to give an example. There is a pine growing throughout northern Europe called the Scots pine by some and the Scotch pine by others. I have seen both of these common names names used in literature. The scientific name of the plant is *Pinus sylvestris*. It is in the genus *Pinus* and is the species *sylvestris*.

The garden of Karel Maly in the Czech Republic shows a wide assortment of conifer cultivars. All these plants were selected by nurserymen and propagated for their special garden attributes. Their origins are as varied as their growth rates, colors, and shapes.

Introduction (cont.)

The scientific name is always underlined when hand written and italicized when printed. The genus is always capitalized while the species is lower case. The difficult thing about the scientific name is its language. Many years ago it was decided to use the language of science, which was Latin. Scientific names are always written in this language with the words used having some descriptive relationship to the plant, either to its appearance or to its discoverer. This scientific name is the same everywhere in the world and is never translated into any other language.

A brief lesson in taxonomy is a necessary evil for anyone wanting to achieve full value from this book. With that in mind, there is just one more very important point about plant names, specifically conifer names.

A cultivar is a species selection that has an attribute that makes it worthy of being grown for use in the garden. This is the third part of the plant name and is written in single quotes. When the plant is propagated and distributed, the cultivar name is then an accepted name. It is not accepted if it only describes one plant that has never been propagated and distributed. This cultivar name can be given to the plant by the first person to either register the name with the Royal Botanic Garden Society or to publish the name with a description in a dated publication that is widely read. Several people have introduced cultivars without validly registering or publishing a name for the plant only to have someone else put a different name on the plant. For example, *Picea glauca* 'Skippack' was a dwarf selection introduced without the name being registered. An author describing this plant in a major publication wrote it as *Picea glauca* 'Cecilia', making the name one that has no relationship at all to the discoverer nor the place of discovery.

By and large, homeowners plant cultivars in their home landscapes. Cultivars are plants that have been grown for special attributes and then named. Anyone can discover a new cultivar by simply being observant and looking for mutations. A cultivar will exhibit a property that is unique and not generally found within the species. A selection may be made because of dwarfness, color, or growth habit. A person may be looking for a plant that stays very small, one that grows along the ground, one that has weeping branches, or one that is a different color than the species. If a selection is made and it is propagated and distributed, then it is considered a cultivar. If it is unique and becomes popular, it may become well known. Otherwise it will soon be lost to cultivation.

The new cultivar may have originated as a seedling mutation or a bud mutation. A seedling mutation occurs when a plant of a species is found that differs in appearance from what might be considered normal for the species. In a sense, all seedlings are mutants since they can show a wide range of variation under normal conditions.

Picea englemannii 'Snake' shows just how far nature can go awry with her mutations. This particular plant is from a spruce species found in the Rocky Mountains but differs from the species norm by its tendency to produce long branches with almost no side buds. It is grotesque in its growth habit but does appeal to many who have seen specimens.

Introduction (cont.)

People who spend time hiking or hunting in wooded areas have opportunities to find unique plants, but these are seldom dwarf plants. Dwarfs cannot compete and are usually killed by the larger plants growing around them. The most common discoveries are color and shape variants. Seedling mutations exist in the wild and may even be found in groupings. Whenever a number of seedling mutations are found in a small area, there must be a unique seed source somewhere nearby.

Conifer seedling nurseries grow millions of seedlings every year. When seedlings are harvested and sorted for shipment, the runts and off-color seedlings are thrown into a trash bin and destroyed. Mutated seedlings are sometimes missed during the sorting process and shipped to growers to be used as understocks for grafting or to be planted out for Christmas trees. As a propagator of grafted conifers, I have learned to watch my potted understocks carefully since color and shape variants do appear from time to time.

People who grow an assortment of conifer cultivars in their landscape will often watch for cone production by their plants. Not all cultivars are sterile, and seed collected from these plants will often develop into a plant that is not at all like the species. Plant societies often sponsor seed exchanges, and conifer seed from cultivars will often produce some interesting plants.

A different class of conifer seedlings has been experimented with since about 1960. These are seedlings grown from witches' brooms. A witches' broom is a bud mutation that develops into an area of congested growth on an otherwise normal tree. The name resulted from the earliest discoveries of witches' brooms. They were, and still are, often found around and in old cemetaries. Superstitious people believed these were places where witches rested when flying through the night skies. Superstition aside, a witches' broom can provide material for propagation that produces a dwarf conifer, provided the broom is genetically changed and not altered due to insect damage or parasitism, usually by mistletoe. Many of the conifer cultivars available today originated from witches' brooms. Some of them bear only a faint resemblance or none at all to the original broom while others are almost identical.

A bud mutation may produce a branch that is very different from its parent tree in shape or color. For example, *Pinus contorta* 'Frisian Gold' has a color and a growth habit that make it a very desirable plant by all who see it. It originated as a bud mutation that created a golden sport.

Sometimes a terminal bud mutates at the end of a branch into exceptionally congested growth. This growth develops into what is referred to as a witches' broom. Sometimes the broom may be found on a young plant while other times it will be on a very old specimen. When pieces of a witches' broom are propagated, a dwarf plant may result. Many of the presently known dwarf conifers were discovered as witches' brooms.

Introduction (cont.)

One of the major problems with selecting a new cultivar is determining whether or not it is a new selection or something that is not much different from previous selections. No matter how a cultivar is selected and named, there may already be a plant in the trade that is very similar, and may even be superior to the new selection. Since no one person knows all of the cultivars in existence at any one time, confusion over the proper names for many garden plants is all too common. Some species have produced so many named cultivars that any attempt to sort everything out is almost hopeless.

In today's world, conifers have become very popular for the garden and as an item to be coveted by collectors. Many people throughout the world have become very active in searching out witches' brooms and seedling mutations. As a result of this activity, new cultivars are appearing at a rate unequaled at anytime in plant history. Few of these new selections are evaluated as to stability and mature size before being released. A large number of these new selections are very similar to cultivars that have already been named and marketed for years. This frenzied activity only adds to the confusion already present in the world of conifers. Not only does the gardener become confused reading a listing that includes many of the newer cultivars, but the expert grower also finds that losing a label spells disaster since many of these new plants are very hard to distinguish.

Throughout this book I will be showing and describing many different cultivars. I will try to guide the reader in a manner that is both informative and non threatening using scientific names.

The garden pictured to the right was developed by Kas Koemans, Boskoop, Holland, who was an avid conifer collector who specialized in *Chamaecyparis* and *Cryptomeria* cultivars.

Small Conifer Landscapes

Everyone has his own definition for miniature conifers, dwarf conifers, and semi-dwarf conifers. So rather than carelessly tossing these terms around or using someone else's random definition, I will use them in this way.

I consider a miniature conifer to be one that will measure less than three feet (one meter) in any one direction after fifteen years of average growth. A dwarf conifer will measure less than six feet (two meters) in any one direction after fifteen years of average growth. A semi-dwarf conifer will measure less than nine feet (three meters) in any one direction after fifteen years of average growth. Under optimum conditions, a conifer may grow faster than is expected so I am considering averages when I classify conifers according to these measurements.

Miniature conifers are very difficult to find in garden centers and are almost impossible to buy in chain stores. There is a good reason for this. Most people associate price with size and want to purchase a large plant for their money. Thus, faster growing plants are the ones most readily available. When the bargain conscious consumer purchases such a plant and treats it as if it were not going to grow much more than it already has, he makes a costly mistake. He now has a plant with a short useful life span.

A miniature conifer has the potential for a very long and useful life in any landscape. It will grow less than three inches per year at its maximum growth rate. Such a plant must be grown several years in the wholesale plant nursery in order to attain a saleable size. The extra years of care require a higher selling price, but remember the old adage "You get what you pay for."

I have always been fascinated with miniature conifers. They are true freaks of nature that have almost no chance of survival without human intervention. When miniature conifers appear in the wild as seedlings, they are quickly strangled by any larger plants growing near them. Any witches' brooms that develop have short life spans since they are rapidly shaded by normally growing branches higher in the tree. However, when used in a landscape, miniatures have a longer life expectancy than most of their companion plants, provided the companion plants are not allowed to crowd them.

Coenosium Gardens

Small Conifer Landscapes (cont.)

I have seen many different forms of miniature conifers. Some grow into tight little cushions while others become miniature trees. Others resemble little globes while some are even shaped like Hershey's Kisses, and some are tight little spires. No matter what the final shape, these plants add variety to any landscape and require very little maintenance when established.

Miniature conifers are perfect for narrow borders, foundation plantings, rock gardens, garden railroads, containers, trough gardens, and as a complement to heather or dwarf perennial gardens. Miniature conifers are often planted in gardens with a few accent plants and a scattering of rocks. No matter how miniature conifers are used in the landscape, they will not outgrow their location and seldom need replacement.

When using miniature conifers in a landscape, first decide where they may be most effective. Obviously they cannot be used as individual specimens or among plants that become large and/or bushy. Also since they will cost more than most conifers, they should be planted where they can be enjoyed on a daily basis. Since they are small, a raised bed will bring them closer to eye level where they may be more readily appreciated.

A raised bed may be created in a number of ways. The simplest raised bed is made with topsoil positioned so that it appears natural. It looks best if it can be developed at the base of a slope, where the topsoil can be graded to appear like a flat, raised projection of the slope itself. The slope can be very slight or more pronounced and still serve nicely to tie the raised bed into the landscape. Walls of native stone can be utilized along portions of the raised areas to allow the visitor closer viewing of the plants by providing definite boundaries and still keep a natural appearance.

If the garden area is not sloped, several tapered mounds can give the impression of natural hummocks, thus preventing an artificial appearance. They need not be large and can be shaped for any size garden. Merely construct them to the scale of the garden. Since these artificial hummocks are to be planted with dwarf conifers, even the small garden will have a natural appearance. In the more formal garden, a raised bed can be created with cottage stones, cut stones, bricks, or treated timbers.

A walkway along a raised bed should always reflect the nature of the raised bed. Raised areas that are intended to be informal may have walkways of grass, gravel, or bark while formal ones will tend to have walkways of flagstone, gravel, or concrete.

Geers garden

Small Conifer Landscapes (cont.)

Miniature conifers are perfect along the top of a low retaining wall. They do not overpower the wall and can be viewed by anyone walking along the front of it. If the wall is constructed of cottage stones or fieldstones, the conifers can be placed more randomly. The cultivars can easily be the ones without formal outlines. On the other hand, if the stones are set in mortar or if the wall is built of brick, a more formal plan using conifers with smoother outlines needs to be followed. If a weeping plant is used above a wall, it can be quite attractive when allowed to grow down the face of the wall. The mound it creates above the wall will break up the straight lines of the wall itself.

Usually a wall is part of a system for terracing a slope. In more formal settings, the landscaped portion might be a narrow band along the top of the wall while the informal setting will often see the slope continuing up from the wall and being completely incorporated into the garden.

Slopes erode and must be planted accordingly. Walls will help prevent erosion but are not always feasible, nor always desired. Covering a slope with a ground cover can prevent erosion but can be less than exciting. Turning the slope into a garden is much more interesting. The size of the slope will determine the type of garden. Most often a variation of a rock garden works best on a slope. The rocks not only provide interest but also help anchor the soil.

Mention the term "rock garden" and someone may picture anything from a pile of rocks with a few plants to a scattering of rocks with many plants. Actually a rock garden is a mixture of plants and rocks arranged to please the owner and allow the plants to do well.

The rocks need not be native to the gardener's locale but should be the kinds that are found together in nature. Do not intermingle native rock such as granite or basalt with limestone. If different kinds are used, they should be used in different areas of the garden. Once selected, the rocks can be placed.

There are no great secrets to the placing of rocks in a rock garden. Merely follow nature. Good pictures of mountain scenery will show rock structures and provide many ideas. Flat rocks naturally appear in layers while glacial rocks are a mixture of many different sizes of rounded rocks. Flat rocks can be used in horizontal layers or tilted into vertical, layered structures while round rocks varying in size and composition may be scattered throughout a garden. Do not use flat rocks and round rocks in the same garden, unless the round rocks are used as part of a streambed, either dry or with flowing water.

Coenosium Rock Garden at South Seattle Community College

Small Conifer Landscapes (cont.)

Rocks should not sit on the surface of the ground. Large individual rocks need to be two-thirds buried as to give the impression of being part of a formation. Align all of the long axes of the rocks in the same direction or in a sweeping curve. The quantity of rock is up to the gardener. I have seen rock gardens that were mostly rock and others that had only a sprinkling of rocks.

Rock garden soil needs to be very well drained and not very rich in humus. Poorer soils mimic alpine soils and will naturally stunt the growth of conifers, keeping them more dwarf than normal without affecting their health. In our rock gardens, the conifers have a healthy color and appearance while growing at about three-fourths their normal rate because they are in glacial subsoil. Since many conifers thrive in organically poor alpine soils throughout the world, such a growth rate is not unexpected.

Careful selection and placement of dwarf and miniature conifers in any rock garden will create a feeling of age and permanence. They need to be carefully positioned since in most cases they will outlive the other plants in the garden. Unlike their species, dwarf and miniature cultivars will not outgrow their sites and take over the garden.

Small, upright conifers can be used in a wide range of settings throughout a rock garden to add year-round variety to a landscape. Large rocks make excellent backdrops for the dwarf, upright plants. Upright plants soften the border between the rock and the garden and balance the height of the rock(s) behind it. As long as the plant is miniature, it will always accent the rocks rather than hide them. Miniature, upright conifers will also add variety to an area of low alpine plants. Miniature conifers offer colors and textures that differ from the alpines and have year round foliage. They will not overgrow the alpines and will stay in scale with the garden.

Alpine meadows will often have a scattering of stunted upright plants as well as plants that have developed into tight, stunted little mounds, usually due to a combination of climate and grazing by herbivores. In the rock garden, these little mounds can be duplicated without the need to import an animal to do the grazing. Many dwarf plants never develop any strong shoots and become cushions and buns. These plants may be scattered through the open areas of the rock garden as a complement to the rocks. Their rounded shapes will either mimic round rocks in a garden or soften the edges of angular rocks. Even a small stream will appear larger if miniature conifers are used.

Esteldorfer garden

Small Conifer Landscapes (cont.)

Miniature conifers are also perfect for container gardens. A container garden is essentially a miniaturized landscape in a trough, pot, barrel, or other artificially constructed container. While other conifers will outgrow their site, the miniatures will stay in scale and allow the artificial landscape to function for many years.

Miniature conifers do need some special considerations when they are part of a landscape. First, miniature conifers need to be sited where they are not overwhelmed by larger plants. Second, they are best displayed in a raised planting for better viewing and protection from physical damage by large or small feet. Third, they need protection from wildlife for many years due to their small size. Fourth, they must have good air circulation to prevent the spread of disease in their typically dense foliage.

Small Conifers for Small Gardens was written to help the reader choose appropriate miniature to dwarf conifers for his garden. By following the suggestions in this book, he may look forward to many years of minimal garden maintenance and maximum garden pleasure.

Iseli Nursery

Krejci garden

Abies concolor 'Archer's Dwarf'

On various trips through Europe I would occasionally come across an attractive blue fir with an almost perfect Christmas tree shape. It always "made a statement" whenever it was a part of the landscape. I learned its name the first time I saw it and knew it immediately every time I came across it again. It is very distinctive in a number of ways.

Abies concolor 'Archer's Dwarf' is a small tree with a narrowly conical growth habit. It has a growth rate of up to 4" (10 cm) per year. The branch structure is very dense with many smaller branchlets. The bright blue needles are long, thin, and sickle-shaped, almost touching across the tops of the branches.

A typical specimen of *Abies concolor* 'Archer's Dwarf' will have a large number of terminal shoots on the branch ends. When these shoots are grafted onto seedlings, they need minimal training to develop into upright little shrubs. 'Archer's Dwarf' grows best in the full sun with well-drained soil. In its native habitat it has adapted to dry soils and cold temperatures, but garden conditions do not always mimic nature.

It is interesting how many selections of the native North American conifer species have been found and named by Europeans. This one was discovered by J. W. Archer, Farnham, Surrey, England about 1982. *Abies concolor* is native to the mountains of western North America, but several excellent selections have been made in European gardens. *Abies concolor* 'Archer's Dwarf' is but one of these.

As a side note, the blue foliage is due to the presence of a powder covering the leaf surfaces. Excessive water and/or wind striking the leaf surfaces will cause the blue to fade with time. Typically a blue conifer has its best color in the late spring and summer before the powder is rubbed/worn off the needle surface.

Linssen garden

Abies concolor 'Piggelmee'

The name of a conifer is a very important aspect of its popularity with gardeners. Unfortunately, some conifers are given names that condemn the plant to obscurity. 'Piggelmee', on the other hand, is a name that produces a variety of favorable mental images and stimulates a gardener's natural curiosity.

Abies concolor 'Piggelmee' is a miniature concolor fir. Every garden has space for one of these beauties, but not every garden has the proper growing conditions for it. Wet winters and springs can cause foliage blights while poorly draining soils will cause root rot. I have excellent conifer soil conditions but have problems growing any of the miniature cultivars of *Abies concolor* due our Northwest climatic conditions.

'Piggelmee' was discovered as a witches' broom on *Abies concolor* 'Candicans' by H. J. Draijer, Heemstede, Holland, sometime before 1972. It is a miniature selection that grows about 1" (3 cm) per year and has an exceptionally dense branching habit.

Abies concolor 'Candicans' has exceptionally bright blue foliage and is very popular in its own right. This color is shared with 'Piggelmee', which has short, thick blue needles that are densely arranged on its short stems. The color and texture of this plant add an attractive aspect to any garden.

'Piggelmee' is often described as a flat, spreading selection of concolor fir. This description is true for a young plant but not necessarily for an older one. I was visiting a conifer collector in Holland a few years ago. As we walked around his garden, I noticed an *Abies concolor* 'Piggelmee' that was about three feet wide and about the same in height. It stood out because his large garden had only three conifers that were over twenty years old, and this was one of them. Five years previously the rest of his collection had been destroyed when he mistakenly sprayed an herbicide onto his plants, thinking it was an insecticide.

Apparently 'Piggelmee' will produce occasional upright shoots that become stunted and heavily branched. This allows the plant to maintain its congested growth habit. That is a good characteristic since it provides contrast in the dwarf conifer garden to the many cushion-shaped dwarf conifers. It also allows 'Piggelmee' to maintain its position in the garden as the garden matures.

Plant *Abies concolor* 'Piggelmee' in well drained soil where it receives full sun and has good air circulation around its foliage.

Beran garden

Kohout garden

Abies koreana 'Blauer Eskimo'

Few fir selections are dwarf with blue foliage. *Abies koreana* 'Blauer Eskimo' is one of the better ones, when grown under favorable conditions.

Commonly found in gardens throughout Europe, *Abies koreana* 'Blauer Eskimo' is used wherever a pale blue cushion is wanted. Growing at the rate of just over 1" (3 cm) per year, 'Blauer Eskimo' develops into a broad mound less than 12" (30 cm) high when it is 24" (60 cm) wide. The foliage is pale blue with gray buds that are partially coated with white resin. It does best in full to partial sun with well drained, fertile soil.

In 1988 I wrote an article about conifer cultivars suitable for grafted standards. My Dutch friend, Wiel Linssen, read it and started doing a variety of dwarf conifers on "stems" as he referred to them. Linssen discovered that one of the nicest selections for doing standards was *Abies koreana* 'Blauer Eskimo'. High grafting brings the plant off the ground for better viewing and provides better air circulation for healthier growth. Wet springs can cause fungal problems on the new foliage of 'Blauer Eskimo', but high grafting helps prevent those problems.

In the summer of 2001 Ronald Vermeulen, another Dutch friend, and I visited the Wittboldt-Muller Nursery in Germany, a nursery known for treating conifer seeds with radiation to create seedling mutations. By this method, they successfully produced *Sciadopitys verticillata* 'Sternschnuppe', with its doubled chromsomes and a number of *Abies koreana* variants.

A major goal of the Wittboldt-Muller Nursery has always been to produce a fast-growing, well-branched, blue form of *Abies koreana* for the Christmas tree industry in Germany. Among their introductions are *Abies koreana* 'Blaue Zwo' and *Abies koreana* 'Blauer Pfiff', two powder blue trees. They are continuously trying to improve these selections by cross pollinating them with blue selections of *Abies lasiocarpa*.

One of the 'Blauer Pfiff' trees provided a surprise for the nursery. A witches' broom appeared on one of its lower branches and had the same bright blue foliage of the parent tree. The 'Blauer Pfiff' was in a block of trees being grown for their seeds. We followed a short trail that had been cut into the block of 'Blauer Pfiff' specimens and found the witches' broom in an area that had been cleared of overhanging limbs. It was not in great shape but was surviving. It is always a treat to see the source of a nice cultivar.

Linssen garden

Esteldorfer garden

Abies koreana 'Gait'

Wiel Linssen, a good Dutch friend of mine, has one of the largest dwarf conifer collections in Europe and will redo portions of his gardens every few years. I always enjoy visiting him because he always has something new in his gardens. During the summer of 2006, I was visiting Wiel when I had noticed a group of *Pinus x schwerinii* 'Wiethorst' growing near the front of his property. As I walked out to the pines, I came across a dense little pillar that was covered with purple cones. I remember thinking, "What a great little treasure for the conifer garden".

Abies koreana 'Gait' is one member of a select group of dwarf conifers that will dependably produce large numbers of cones on a regular basis. It grows just over 3" (8 cm) per year, is densely branched, and develops into a narrow little pillar. The foliage is dark green and small, blue cones are produced in large numbers.

Cone production takes place as a conifer matures and can require up to twenty or more years to commense, although an individual plant may actually produce cones at a younger age. For example, seedlings of *Picea abies* 'Acrocona' will cone as young as five years. When any conifer becomes mature enough to produce cones, propagations of that conifer will also produce cones because the age of the parent tree is carried forth in each of the propagations. Dwarf conifers that produce cones generally do so because they originated as witches' brooms on older trees that had attained maturity.

Grafted plants of *Abies koreana* 'Gait' are very slow to develop any size. It will never become a common selection in garden centers, but, nonetheless, is a valuable asset to any garden. The slow growth rate coupled with its extensive cone production results in an attractive addition to any landscape.

Abies koreana 'Gait' was introduced in 1975 by Roelvink Nursery, Zuidbroek, Holland, where it originated as a seedling. It is an uncommon plant throughout Europe and may be seen only in conifer collectors' gardens. Locating one for sale does require contacting specialty nurseries and will probably require mail order purchasing.

Linssen garden

Abies koreana 'Kohout's Icebreaker'

One of the most exciting plants to make an appearance in gardens during the 1980's was *Abies koreana* 'Horstmann's Silberlocke'. Gunter Horstmann introduced this plant under that name in 1979, and it rapidly became very popular. All the needles curl and expose their silvery undersides producing an effect similar to a flocked Christmas tree.

Jorg Kohout, a German nurseryman/conifer collector, found a witches' broom on a 'Horstmann's Silberlocke' and propagated it. What resulted is one of the most exciting new conifers to appear in a long time. Imagine a ball of silver growing in your garden. *Abies koreana* 'Kohout's Icebreaker' has the same needle curl as the tree of its origin, but the curl is much more pronounced and more dependable. This fact is not too surprising since 'Horstmann's Silberlocke' maintains its curl best when it is kept under some stress, and 'Kohout's Icebreaker' is a mutation that produces extensive branching and slow growth, the equivalent to a 'Horstmann's Silberlocke' under stress.

Jorg Kohout's garden is a treasure trove of dwarf and miniature conifers. He has planted something in every available square meter of his property. Being a nurseryman, his goal is to compare these small growing treasures under the same growing conditions and to make selections for his nursery business. *Abies koreana* 'Kohout's Icebreaker' is obviously a winner. He had this plant scattered in various locations throughout his garden at different levels. Several were growing as mounds upon the ground while others were grafted as standards at a wide range of heights. 'Kohout's Icebreaker' does best in fertile soil with full sun. Poor air circulation and cold, wet weather in the spring can cause some difficulties with foliar diseases.

Young plants are consistently globose and densely branched with curved needles displaying their silvery undersides so extensively that the bark on the young branches is completely hidden. The growth rate is up to 1" (3 cm) per year for its branchlets and just under 2" (5 cm) per year for the branches. As a plant develops, it may produce an upright shoot and develop more of an upright habit, all the while staying very dense, dwarf, and above all, very silver in color. In that way it may prove to have a growth habit very similar to that of *Abies koreana* 'Silberperle'.

This plant won't be readily available for a number of years since it was first offered for sale in quantity in 2009. For now, only a few specialty nurseries will offer it for sale. It is easy to propagate, but its high demand will always affect availability.

For the best results it is commonly propagated by grafting. In the future it may prove to readily root from cuttings. *Abies koreana* 'Horstmann's Silberlocke', the parent plant, easily roots from cuttings and slowly develops into a dense, symmetrical little bush that takes some time to assume its normal tree-like growth rate.

Linssen garden

Linssen garden

Abies koreana 'Silberkugel'

Europeans have been proficient at finding witches' brooms and stunted seedlings of *Abies koreana*. Quite a few selections have been found and named that are reliably dwarf or miniature. Some of them are susceptible to fungal problems in a cool, wet spring; others are not. These selections include *Abies koreana* 'Pinocchio' (seedling selection by the Carstens Baumschule, Germany), *Abies koreana* 'Nadelkissen' (seedling selection from the Wittbolt-Müller Nursery, Germany), *Abies koreana* 'Kohout's Hexe'(witches' broom found by Jorge Kohout, Germany), and *Abies koreana* 'Kristallkugel' (witches' broom found at the Wittbolt-Müller Nursery, Germany). Their growth habits are all similar, and young plants can be difficult to distinguish by the average person.

Abies koreana 'Silberkugel' is a miniature plant that is easy to distinguish from the members of this select group. Growing about 1" (3 cm) per year, 'Silberkugel' has a mass of branchlets that appear to spread horizontally over the top of the plant. Each branchlet is slightly curved with the foliage concentrated more toward its tip. The older branchlets are beneath the younger ones as the plant dependably grows into the shape of a broadly spreading cushion. The needles have a slight twist, producing a bicolored effect of silver and green.

When I first added this plant to my collection, it was under the name 'Hexenbesen Wustemeyer No. 1' and consisted of three little pieces of wood in a small plastic bag. Three years later I realized that I had a real winner to add to my conifer collection. It is best grown in bright sunlight with some shade during the heat of the afternoon, otherwise an exceptionally hot summer afternoon could cause foliage burn if the ground dries out. Planting *Abies koreana* 'Silberkugel' in well drained, fertile soil will help it thrive.

I have never met Werner Wustemeyer, but he did find and introduce a number of outstanding cultivars. *Abies koreana* 'Lippetall' (formerly called 'Zwergform Wustemeyer') is another exceptional plant, but I must control myself or this book will become two volumes! 'Lippetall' is a densely branched, columnar selection that grows just over 2" (5 cm) per year with dark green foliage and is also very suitable for the smaller garden.

Abies koreana 'Silberkugel'
Coenosium Gardens

Abies koreana 'Kristallkugel'
Vermeulen garden

Abies koreana 'Silberperle'

From the early 1960's through the 1980's the name Gunter Horstmann was synonymous with the term hexenbesen (witches' broom), and both were often used in the same sentence. Horstmann lived in Schneverdingen, Germany, and introduced an extensive number of new conifers to the gardening world. Firs and spruces were his special forte. One of his many choice introductions was a plant with the initial name of *Abies koreana* 'Horstmann Hexebesen', a temporary designation until a better name could be chosen.

Abies koreana 'Silberperle' originated from a hexenbesen that was found and propagated by Horstmann. The broom was a 5" (13 cm) ball in a 5' (2.6 m) tall tree. When grafted, it grew about 2" (5 cm) per year. 'Silberperle' is spherical when young with short, thick branches that produce numerous buds, which, in turn, develop into stubby branchlets. The foliage is green with enough twist to the needles to give the plant an almost silver and green bicolored appearance. As it ages, 'Silberperle' will develop a terminal shoot, becoming more conical while still maintaining its dense branch structure. The terminal shoot can grow up to 3" (8 cm) per year.

As the new growth hardens off through the end of summer, the buds mature into little spheres along the branches and branchlets. They are covered with white resin and take on the appearance of tiny pearls thoughout the plant, thus the name 'Silberperle'.

This selection does well in the full sun but must not be allowed to dry out during a hot summer afternoon. That would cause foliage burn. As it becomes larger, the chance of burning becomes much less. The soil should be fertile and well drained but still able to retain some moisture.

As often happens, other dwarf forms of *Abies koreana* appeared in the years following the introduction of 'Silberperle'. *Abies koreana* 'Silberzwerg' and 'Silber Mavers' are two forms that grow identical to 'Silberperle'. They are either the same plant with other names or originated independently of 'Silberperle' and just happen to be identical to it. Either way, those names should not be used since they merely add to the world of "taxonomic confusion".

Coenosium Gardens

Esteldorfer garden

Abies lasiocarpa 'Alpine Beauty'

Miniature and dwarf conifers come in an assortment of sizes and shapes. Most commonly the shape is cushionlike to globose. Upright or conical growth habits are fairly rare so when a conical shaped plant is discovered that has garden merit, it quickly develops wide appeal among gardeners.

Jerry Morris is known for his work with witches' brooms in conifers throughout the mountains of western North America. One of his best finds was a broom on *Abies lasiocarpa* that has been developed and given the name 'Alpine Beauty'.

Abies lasiocarpa 'Alpine Beauty' is globose as a young plant but soon becomes conical as it ages. The silvery-blue foliage has a soft appearance with a shiny luster. It is densely branched with the needles hiding the branch structure. Growing less than 2" (5 cm) per year, it will be about 12" (30 cm) tall in ten years.

This plant was introduced to the nursery trade by Larry Stanley of Boring, Oregon, through a program he developed with Morris. Another *Abies lasiocarpa* introduced at the same time was 'Prickley Pete'. This cultivar deceptively starts out looking like a young 'Alpine Beauty'. But it originated from a tree that was over 10' (3 m) tall and about 12" (30 cm) across and had short branches covering the trunk, giving the appearance of a cactus. I am still waiting for the upright growth habit to manifest itself in the garden.

Grafting is the best method for propagating *Abies lasiocarpa* 'Alpine Beauty'. Its soft foliage will tend to suffer blighted spots in the late spring and early summer if weather conditions are exceptionally wet and cold. During drier weather the spots soon disappear, and the overall plant is little affected.

This plant benefits from good air circulation and full sun exposure. The soil needs the good drainage required for most firs. Using the plant among faster growing perennials is not recommended since it would be too crowded. An open area like a rock garden would be a perfect setting. As the name indicates, it is an 'Alpine Beauty'.

Coenosium Gardens

Abies lasiocarpa 'DuFlon'

Abies lasiocarpa 'DuFlon' is a miniature fir with an interesting story. In 1954 Alton and Bita DuFlon were hiking near Lake Cushman on the Olympic Peninsula when they came across a congested, little tree that must have been over 100 years old. They were able to successfully transplant this little treasure to their home in Seattle, Washington. Within a few years, this plant came to the attention of Ed Lohbrunner, the owner of Lakeside Gardens, a nursery specializing in alpine plants in Victoria, British Columbia. Lohbrunner would periodically visit the DuFlons attempting to obtain propagation material from this diminutive fir. Eventually the DuFlons allowed Lohbrunner to take three small pieces from the miniature tree. He was able to root the three pieces and grew them on with the idea of using them as stock plants.

The original tree only lived a few years and died. It is uncertain as to what caused its death, and a strange story was started by someone unknown. According to urban legend, another woman was involved in the discovery of the original plant. She and the DuFlons had an argument over the tree after it was planted on the DuFlon property. To settle the argument the tree was cut in half in order to share it. Both halves died. When I met Bita DuFlon in 1989, she told me how upset she became whenever she heard that story. As a professional gardener she would never have done such a foolish thing. I still come across that story from time to time and hope that this account will "bury it".

Lohbrunner was able to produce the plant and eventually offer it for sale. It is now available from specialty nurseries. Some discussion has occurred as to the correct name for this plant: 'Duflon', 'Du Flon', or 'DuFlon'. In checking public records I found Alton DuFlon's name to be a single word in his obituary and in publications he worked on for Boeing so I believe *Abies lasiocarpa* 'DuFlon' to be the correct spelling for this wonderful little plant.

Developing into a congested little tree as it ages, *Abies lasiocarpa* 'DuFlon' is a miniature mound that is a bun for many years, until a weak leader establishes itself, then it will gain a little height. Growing about .5" (1 cm) per year it needs many years to even show a sign of a weak leader. Its foliage consists of green needles that are very tiny, staying in scale with the size of the plant.

Abies lasiocarpa 'DuFlon' can be propagated from cuttings or by grafting. The growth rate is slightly faster when grafted, but after a few years it reverts back the same rate as a cutting-grown plant.

The alpine garden is a perfect place for *Abies lasiocarpa* 'DuFlon'. It will be a small, dense cushion for many years and is much too slow to outgrow its space. It is also an excellent choice for a trough or container garden. It does well in full sun and needs well drained soil.

Coenosium Gardens

Abies lasiocarpa 'Lopalpun'

Gunter Horstmann used to spend considerable time traveling in western North America searching for witches' brooms. He found several in his travels that have proven to be exceptional. A number of these brooms were on *Abies lasiocarpa*. Two of them are very similar, and both may be found in gardens throughout Europe and North America.

Abies lasiocarpa 'Logan Pass' and *Abies lasiocarpa* 'Lopalpun' are almost identical, but 'Lopalpun' performs better in the garden setting since 'Logan Pass' appears to be more susceptible to fungal attack during prolonged wet spells.

Abies lasiocarpa 'Lopalpun' is a dense, miniature globe with stubby branches, each having several large buds at its terminus and numerous small buds scattered along each branch. It grows less than 1" (3 cm) per year. The foliage is almost a slate gray color with the needles being very small and thinly scattered on each branch and densely clustered around the terminal buds. A plant in the garden will appear to be a solid mass of foliage due to the impenetrable number of branches packed tightly together.

Older plants maintain their globose shapes as they grow, making 'Lopalpun' a dependable member of the landscape. For the best results, 'Lopalpun' should be planted in well drained soil with lots of sunlight and good air circulation.

Abies lasiocarpa 'Lopalpun' is best propagated by grafting onto *Abies procera* seedlings. I prefer to use *Abies procera* because other species tend to form thick callous tissue at the graft site, creating an unsightly mass just above the soil line.

Abies lasiocarpa 'Lopalpun'
Coenosium Gardens

Abies lasiocarpa 'Logan Pass'
Beran garden

Abies nordmanniana 'Golden Spreader'

Sir Harold Hillier is a name that is spoken with reverence by English gardeners. From the 1950's to the present time his nursery has been at the center of the horticultural world. During his life time, he set a high standard for others to follow. The dwarf conifer collection at the main house is now part of the Hillier Arboretum and is maintained by a foundation.

In the late 1970's I was visiting the Hillier Arboretum to see the dwarf conifer collection when I came across a dense, broadly conical shrub with bright gold foliage. I found a label that indicated the plant was *Abies nordmanniana* 'Golden Spreader', a plant I had never seen before. I now have this plant scattered throughout my own gardens. It provides a bright spot in the landscape wherever it is grown. During the winter the color intensifies.

I was concerned about the possibility of sunscald due to some plants I had seen at the National Dwarf Conifer Collection in Windsor Great Park, Windsor, England. There was a grouping of three young plants growing in the full sun that had been badly burned. In my own garden I would occasionally notice burn in the early spring, but it was always quickly covered up by the new season's growth. As my plants became established, any sign of sunscald became a rarity. I have two mature specimens on the west side of our house that are problem free.

Abies nordmanniana 'Golden Spreader' is a dwarf, dense, broadly conical plant that grows about 3" (6 cm) per year. Its foliage is yellow-green in the spring, becoming bright golden yellow through the summer. It is susceptible to sun scald in full exposure in young plants. I have several in partial shade that turn bright yellow in the winter in spite of the lower light levels. Full shade, however, reduces the color's intensity.

Abies nordmanniana 'Golden Spreader' originated as a seedling about 1961 in the nursery of S. N. Shoots, Culemborg, near Boskop, Holland. Although young plants are spreading in habit, each one will eventually develop a slow growing terminal shoot and develop the shape of an old fashioned honey bee hive.

Since it will become large for the smaller garden, 'Golden Spreader' is a borderline plant for this book. However, its color and shape make it very desirable for any garden that can use a plant which may be 6' (2 m) tall and 8' (2.6 m) wide in twenty years. It can be utilized as a minispecimen in smaller sized landscapes or as part of a border garden among perennials as long as the perennials are not allowed to shade its lower branches.

Abies nordmaniana 'Golden Spreader'
Coenosium Gardens

Abies procera 'Blaue Hexe'

Abies procera, commonly called the noble fir, is a popular Christmas tree, and some selections have been made for shape and color. One large tree with striking blue color is *Abies procera* 'Glauca'. Another selection is *Abies procera* 'Glauca Prostrata' which is described as a blue tree that grows like a carpet. This selection is actually a cultivariant produced by grafting lateral branches from 'Glauca'. Since *Abies* exhibit plagiotropism and tend to grow horizontally for a number of years before sending up a terminal shoot, procumbent and prostrate cultivars are generally flat-growing only because they are propagated from lateral shoots and will eventually put up a leader.

Abies procera 'Blaue Hexe' originated as a congested growth in a tree. This type of congested growth is known as a witches' broom (hexenbesen in German). Discovered by the Boehlje Nursery, Westerstede, Germany, in 1965, 'Blaue Hexe' is a dwarf selection that grows broad and globose with short branches and bright blue, short, wide needles. It will grow up to 2" (5 cm) per year.

During the early 1980's while traveling with Dick van Hoey Smith in Holland visiting conifer collectors and their gardens, I first saw 'Blaue Hexe'. Every garden had one or more plants of this cultivar used in a variety of ways. The most memorable use was as a specimen on the top of a low stone block wall in the garden of Wiel Linssen. The intensely blue foliage made a dramatic contrast with the dark gray stone of the wall as well as with a number of golden conifers in the immediate area.

I have at least ten 'Blaue Hexe' scattered through our three acres of gardens. They require little space in the garden and add much color. As young plants they are low-spreading cushions, developing some upward growth as they age. As time passes, they will make more of a statement in the garden but will not outgrow their locations.

Abies procera 'Blaue Hexe' is propagated by grafting onto true fir (*Abies*) seedlings. I prefer to use *Abies procera* seedlings since other seedling species often produce callous tissue along the graft union creating an ugly looking graft.

Linssen garden

Vermeulen garden

The *Abies veitchii* Triumvirate

Three exceptional cultivars have been selected and named from *Abies veitchii*. The *veitchii* foliage is especially attractive, and each has special attributes that makes it a fine choice for the smaller garden. When planted under the proper conditions, the plant will thrive. I have been growing several plants of each cultivar in various locations in our gardens. I have found that under dry conditions *veitchii* cultivars do not have a very good appearance. They seem to do best in richer soil with some protection from the hot afternoon sun when kept moderately moist. These demands are quite different from the typical fir.

Found as a witches' broom in Hamburg, Germany, before 1985, *Abies veitchii* 'Heddergott' is the largest growing of these three selections. It begins as a low, dense, spreading bush. As it ages, it becomes vase-shaped with a depressed center and ascending branches with short, green needles that are slightly twisted, exposing their silvery undersides. The growth rate also accelerates as it ages to about 3" (8 cm) per year.

Abies veitchii 'Rumburk' is a dense, miniature, nest-forming selection with a slightly irregular outline. According to its discoverer, at twenty-five years it will be about 20" (55cm) wide by 28" (60cm) high. In the Northwest, however, it grows about 3" (8 cm) per year and seems to grow broader than high. Its foliage is silver and blue-gray due to exposure of the undersides of many of the needles which have a blue-gray surface color. 'Rumburk' originated from a witches' broom discovered in 1972 near Rumburk, Czech Republic, by Ladizslav Fritsche.

The third cultivar of this special group, *Abies veitchii* 'Heine', is a dwarf, spreading plant. Growing up to 3" (8 cm) per year with occasional end branches of up to 4" (10 cm), it is similar to 'Heddergott' but with longer leaves and a lighter green color. It was found by W. Wustemeyer, Schermbeck, Germany, about 1991.

'Heddergott' in the Linssen garden

'Heine' to the left and 'Rumburk' above are both in the Vermeulen garden

Cedrus atlantica 'Lilliput'

Ivan Arneson lived on the outskirts of Canby, Oregon, and was known for his azaleas. Conifers were a sideline for his nursery, and he had a knack for finding unusual ones from time to time. Whenever he found a different conifer, he would contact John Mitsch and Mitsch would grow and evaluate it. About 1970 Arneson gave Mitsch a seedling of *Cedrus atlantica*, which was kept in a large container for many years. Now, in 2011, it is just over 10' (3 m) tall by 6' (2 m) wide and growing in a landscaped setting.

The dwarfness and slow growth rate of *Cedrus atlantica* 'Lilliput' result in a rather dense branch structure and create a broadly conical plant with a very interesting texture. It is a compact, open bush with many branchlets and will grow to about 3' (1 m) in ten years. The gray-green foliage is quite sparse along the recent year's growth, and the branchlets have a slight upward curve and are relatively thick.

This plant will make a statement in just about any landscape. It does best in the full sun and is reasonably winter hardy. Since it is an upright form, it can compete with other plants. When it develops some size after a number of years, pruning the branches to expose a view of the trunk will show a trunk diameter usually reserved for trees three times its height. That creates a nice effect, especially in an alpine setting.

Coenosium Gardens

Coenosium Gardens

Cedrus atlantica 'Mount Saint Catherine'

In the spring of 1992 I visited a few conifer friends in New Zealand and Australia. I was gathering information on conifer introductions from that part of the world and determining what I might be able to bring into the United States to make part of my collection. Leo Coolwyn of Monbulk and Ron Radford of Tasmania were my hosts in Australia, and the three of us spent a week traveling throughout the area around Victoria. One of the nicest plants I saw was growing along steps in Coolwyn's back yard.

Cedrus atlantica 'Mount Saint Catherine', a witches' broom discovered and introduced by Peter Taverna at Crafters, South Australia, in 1977, was forming a blue mat and sending tendrils toward the top of a low stone wall. It is a very compact, prostrate, slow-growing plant with exceptionally short, blue needles that develops an irregular outline with some branchlets slightly ascending.

Becoming about 20" (50 cm) wide by 8" (20 cm) high after ten years 'Mount Saint Catherine' can easily develop dead areas of foliage if the proper preventative care is not taken. It is necessary to periodically remove any clusters of dead, older needles.

I was able to bring five young plants of *Cedrus atlantica* 'Mount Saint Catherine' back with me and had an interesting time with the USDA as I reentered the United States. I had to leave the plants with them in Los Angeles, and they mailed them to me after they completed their inspection. Meanwhile, I couldn't believe some of the activity at the airport while I was waiting in line. For example, one person had a suitcase full of "rotting" fruit, and when it was opened for inspection, thousands of fruit flies filled the air causing widespread panic.

'Mount Saint Catherine' has proven to be a difficult plant to establish in gardens here in the Northwest. It does very well as a young plant when grown in a container but suffers when it is planted into the ground. I suspect our wet season from November through April causes stress and resultant fungal problems.

Koelwyn garden

Linssen garden

Cedrus brevifolia 'Kenwith'

Cedrus brevifolia 'Kenwith' is one of those dwarf conifers that has a special attribute to set it apart from most. It is a miniature upright.

Kenwith Castle is the home and nursery of Gordon Haddow, an avid Scottish conifer collector who has introduced a number of new cultivars into the nursery trade. His private pinetum is extensively planted with many rare conifers. He also worked with Humphrey Welch making it possible for Welch to have his extensive conifer cultivar data published in the form of a paperback book.

Cedrus brevifolia 'Kenwith' develops into a miniature, upright tree with a dense branching habit. The branches all grow upward and the tiny, dark green needles become shorter and denser toward their tips. The growth rate is about 2" (5 cm) per year.

Garden railroads are becoming popular throughout the country, and this particular little tree is perfect for this type of landscape use. A train can actually pass through a living forest of trees that are in perfect scale to the whole scheme. However, since this is a *Cedrus brevifolia*, 'Kenwith' is not suitable for zone 6 and colder (USDA hardiness zones).

Taxonomists have recently changed the species of *Cedrus atlantica* and *Cedrus brevifolia* into subspecies of *Cedrus libani*. As a horticulturalist, I will continue to list them as species. Taxonomists tend to make nomenclatural changes with an apparent lack of concern for the nurseryman who tries to keep things up to date. They have their reasons for making these changes, but they tend to confuse the rest of us.

Coenosium Gardens

Vermeulen garden

The Canadian Bonanza of William Goddard

Gordon Bentham, a good Canadian friend, was very close to William Goddard in Victoria, British Columbia. Goddard owned Floravista Gardens and had a flare for finding very special plants. He was especially good at discovering and introducing selections of *Cedrus deodara*. Bentham, on the other hand, was adept at spreading Goddard's discoveries among conifer collectors in the United States. Three of Goddard's dwarf *Cedrus* discoveries were very similar in color but differed in growth rates.

When Bentham shared these three plants with Iseli Nursery in Boring, Oregon, and Mitsch Nursery in Aurora, Oregon, they were quickly put into production. Bentham also sent the plants to me in Pennsylvania, but hardiness was a problem. I soon realized that if I wanted to grow *Cedrus deodara*, Dianne and I would have to move to a milder climate. One summer we visited the Northwest and discovered where that milder climate would be.

When I first visited Bentham in the early 1980's, he showed me Goddard's original *Cedrus deodara* discoveries. Many of these were large trees and included *Cedrus deodara* "Gold Cone', 'Deep Cove', 'Klondyke', and 'Cream Puff', the most successful of almost twenty larger growing *Cedrus* introductions. The three plants described here are not only dwarf, but also possess white foliage that tolerates full sun after the plants are established in the landscape.

Cedrus deodara 'Silver Mist' is the largest growing of the three but is still a dwarf plant, becoming broadly conical with age. The branches are gracefully pendulous and densely clothe a mature plant. It will grow up to 6" (15 cm) per year, but a thirty year old plant may be only 9' (3 m) high and 6' (2 m) wide. The foliage of 'Silver Mist' is white with a green tinge toward the center of the plant, and it may suffer some burn in the full sun as a young plant or during exceptionally dry spells. It was discovered as a seedling by William Goddard about 1964.

(continued)

Cedrus deodara 'Deep Cove'
Coenosium Gardens

The Canadian Bonanza of William Goddard (cont.)

About the same time, possibly in the same seed batch, Goddard found two other white seedlings. One of them, *Cedrus deodara* 'Snow Sprite', is a dense, small bush or mound that grows about 4" (10 cm) per year. Its white foliage may burn in the full sun, but the green tint toward the interior of the plant helps to prevent sunscald, except under the harshest conditions

The third and most dwarf of the three white seedlings, *Cedrus deodara* 'White Imp' is an almost miniature plant that becomes a small pyramid as it ages. Its growth rate is about 3" (7 cm) per year. Its foliage is white and subject to the same limitations as the other two plants described here.

Although these cedars can take full sun, adverse conditions can cause occasional scalding. Interestingly, partial shade seems to actually enhance the whiteness of the foliage. Keeping these two observations in mind, I would recommend using them in the garden where some afternoon shade is available. Barring that, I would make certain they are reliably irrigated. They work very well with other colors and add a splash of brightness to any conifer or flower garden. They also work well as focal points in the smaller garden.

Cedrus deodara 'Silver Mist'
Stanley & Sons Nursery

Cedrus deodara 'Snow Sprite'
Iseli Nursery

Cedrus deodara 'White Imp' Coenosium
Rock Garden at
South Seattle Community College

Cedrus deodara 'Mountain Beauty' and Cedrus deodara 'Scott'

During my visit to Australia in 1992, I spent several days with Don Teese, of Yamina Rare Plants., which was begun by his father, Arnold Teese. At the time they were best known for the introduction of *Cupressus macrocarpa* 'Greenstead Magnificent', which many nurseries described as a blue, dwarf form. Don showed me one of his oldest plants. It was in excess of thirty feet (ten meters) across and almost six feet (two meters) high.

As we walked through his gardens, I noticed a number of whitish *Cedrus deodara* specimens growing throughout one area. They were all wider than high with varying degrees of uniqueness. Don had collected them from various sources and was offering them for sale through the Yamina Rare Plants retail division, which was his area of responsibility. They all originated as witches' brooms discovered in different parts of Australia.

Don generously gave me five young plants of each cultivar that I brought back to America with me. Two of them are described and pictured here. They are more readily available, perhaps because they have proven the easiest to grow in our climate. I have included short descriptions of the others since they all came to America as a group. All five are nice plants and make excellent assets to any smaller garden, but it may prove difficult to find all of them available in any one place.

Cedrus deodara 'Mountain Beauty' is a selection that becomes an irregularly shaped plant with compact foliage. Its foliage has a slight yellowish tinge that sometimes takes on a cream-like color. It will grow up to about 5" (12 cm) per year. It was discovered as a witches' broom in the Blue Mountains west of Sydney, Australia, by Gordon Wilton and introduced by Miltons Nursery of New South Wales about 1985.

Cedrus deodara 'Scott' is a low-growing plant, becoming much wider than high with upward arching, thin branches and thin, sparse needles. It may grow as much as 4" (10 cm) per year. Its color is like that of 'Mountain Beauty'. It was found as a witches' broom at Upper Sturt, South Australia, in 1977 by Peter Taverna.

Cedrus deodara 'Mylor' develops into a dense, mushroom-shaped plant. *Cedrus deodara* 'Waverly Ridge' is a distinctly pendulous selection that changes from a mushroom shape when young to a fountain-like shape when mature. *Cedrus deodara* 'Lime Glow' grows like a miniature, spreading plant for a number of years but does appear to revert, growing upright as it ages and becoming more open with pendulous branches.

Use these plants in the smaller garden where pendulous mounds of cream colored foliage will make the best contrast with the various shades of green.

Cedrus deodara 'Scott'
Coenosium Gardens

Cedrus deodara
'Mountain Beauty'
Stanley & Sons Nursery

Cedrus deodara 'Pygmy' ('Pygmaea')

I have a few concerns about including Cedrus deodara *'Pygmy'. It is a beautiful plant when properly grown, but at the same time it can be difficult to keep it looking attractive. 'Pygmy' is a miniature, dense, globular to squatly conical plant. Its foliage is blue-green and densely arranged along the branchlets. Dead, brown foliage is retained inside the plant due to its dense branching habit. I first saw this plant growing at Mitsch Nursery in Aurora, Oregon. It was one of John Mitsch's favorites, and he propagated it from cuttings with moderate success. I have always had greater success propagating it by grafting. Mitsch moved five stock plants from the nursery to his new home. They were over twenty years old and only 24" (75 cm) wide by 18" (50 cm) high. All five died from the transplant shock.*

Cedrus deodara 'Pygmy' grows less than 1" (2 cm) per year. Due to congested branching and dense foliage, it is susceptible to sunscald and disease problems. Found by James Noble in a California nursery in 1943, it was willed to William Gotelli, New Jersey, in 1958. Later it became part of the Gotelli Dwarf Conifer Collection at the U.S. National Arboretum when Gotelli donated his large conifer collection to the arboretum.

There has been some controversy over the identity of this plant since the Gotelli specimen has always grown faster than the specimens grown in later years on the West Coast. Mitsch got his original Cedrus deodara 'Pygmy' from the Gotelli collection, and Mitsch Nursery became the source for this plant in the nursery trade. It has always been a rare conifer due to its slow growth rate and disease susceptibility. However, when it is well grown and develops some size, it becomes a real treasure in the garden.

Use Cedrus deodara 'Pygmy' in sunny locations with some afternoon shade and good air circulation. Put it in its permanent home and try not to disturb it once it is established.

There is another plant that grows slightly faster than 'Pygmaea' without the blue foliage. Cedrus deodara 'Hollandia' has fewer problems and grows about twice as fast but is still quite small after ten or more years.

'Hollandia' is a true dwarf with short, stiff branches creating a dense, congested plant that is as broad as high. It grows about 2" (5 cm) per year with gray-green foliage having needles that are shorter than the species. It was introduced by Mitsch Nursery about 1985. Mitsch had purchased his original plant from Hollandia Nursery, Modesto, California. I believe his purchase was for the original seedling since Mitsch introduced it into the nursery trade.

Cedrus deodara 'Pygmy'

Cedrus deodara 'Pygmy'
Iseli Nursery

Cedrus libani 'Comte de Dijon'

Cedrus libani is the hardiest of the species of true cedar. That is not to say that it is hardy enough for the upper midwestern United States, but it can be grown where *atlantica* and *deodara* are marginal. Some selections develop into moderately sized shrubs and may be used in smaller gardens. One of the oldest of these is a dense, compact, broadly globular bush named *Cedrus libani* 'Comte de Dijon'. It has dark green foliage with relatively straight needles that are thin at the ends and broad in the center. It grows about 5" (12 cm) per year. Originating at Barbier Nursery, Orleans, France, in 1908, the original plant found its way to the National Botanic Garden, Glasnevin, Dublin, Ireland. In the 1970's it had a height of 16' (5 m) and a width of 12' (4 m). Those are large measurements for a dwarf conifer, but by then it was almost seventy years old.

There are two other cultivars of *Cedrus libani* that are very similar to 'Comte de Dijon' but differ in a number of ways and can be used in the same manner in most landscapes. One of these, *Cedrus libani* 'Nana', is a dense, globose bush with dark green foliage made up of slightly curved needles widely spaced and regularly arranged along its branches. 'Nana' grows about 6" (15 cm) per year. Older than *Cedrus libani* 'Comte de Dijon', 'Nana' originated in England before 1838.

Cedrus libani 'Taurus' is also a dwarf bush that will apparently grow wider than high. It grows about 2" (6 cm) per year with dark green foliage and straight needles. It is a seedling selection made by A. A. M. Vergeer, Boskoop, Holland, about 1988.

Although 'Taurus' grows wider than high and the other two are more upright, all three have similar uses in the garden. They are all slow growing shrubs.

Cedrus libani 'Nana'

Cedrus libani 'Comte de Dijon'
Coenosium Gardens

Cedrus libani 'Green Prince'

Cedrus libani is considered a subspecies of *Cedrus atlantica* by taxonomists. Since taxonomists do not own nurseries and do not realize how confused homeowners become when established names are changed, I will stay with the older designation.

In the late 1960's Neil Hall of Wells Nursery in Mt. Vernon, Washington, found two small *Cedrus libani* growing in a row of *Cedrus libani* trees in Oregon. While talking to the landowner, he discovered that they were all the same age. He took cuttings from the smaller plant and propagated them. The growth rate remained very slow, and they developed into small shrubs. Years later Hall returned to the original site only to discover the original plant had been removed. The other small one was still there, but now it was a tree! Needless to say, it was never propagated.

During the following years, many people thought both plants had been propagated and given two different names - *Cedrus libani* 'Green Prince' and *Cedrus libani* 'Green Knight'. According to Hall, he only propagated one selection, *Cedrus libani* 'Green Prince'. The only 'Green Knight' growing at Wells Nursery is a *Picea orientalis* that becomes a large tree.

Cedrus libani 'Green Prince' is a dwarf plant with congested foliage along twisted branches. If left untouched, it will become dense with age. Alternatively, it can develop an alpine appearance with a minimum of pruning and shaping. 'Green Prince' grows about 1" (2 cm) per year and has very short, dark green needles.

Hardier than many of the true cedars, *Cedrus libani* 'Green Prince' has a number of uses in the landscape. In the colder climates it should have some protection from drying winds and the harsh winter sun. It grows best in sunny locations with well drained soil. Use it in the garden where a dwarf, conical shrub with an irregular outline makes the best impression. It can be used in an oriental type of garden or as a member of an alpine type of garden where it can be given a windswept look.

South Seattle Community College

Cedrus libani 'Sargentii'

Not all of the plants used in a small garden need to be dwarf. *Cedrus libani* 'Sargentii' is one such plant. The name 'Sargentii' is a common plant name in the horticultural world. There is a good reason for that. Charles Sprague Sargent was the first director of the Arnold Arboretum just outside of Boston, Massachusetts, and served for over fifty years. He was the driving force behind its establishment in 1882 as the first arboretum in America when it merged with the city of Boston. During his tenure at the Arnold Arboretum until his death in 1927, Sargent worked with E.H. Wilson and Alfred Rehder to greatly influence the horticultural world with many new plant introductions into American gardens. Through this work, his name became part of many of the new plant names.

Originating in the Arnold Arboretum, Jamaica Plain, Massachusetts, in 1919, *Cedrus libani* 'Sargentii' is a dense, prostrate selection that mounds to a height of about 2' (60 cm). Its branches are numerous and are covered with dark green, long, thick needles. Its growth rate is about 5" (12 cm) per year.

'Sargentii' is most effective when used on a slope, especially in a rock garden, where it can wander among the rocks. It is also effective on an elevation next to a water feature or at the top of a stone wall. In all of these locations its prostrate growth habit adds to the garden's hardscape. It survives in harsher climates since it will often be protected by winter snow.

The picture at the right was taken in the garden of Marty Brooks in Pennsylvania. It is a very old specimen. Brooks specialized in the sale of old, mature specimens of conifers and deciduous trees. I first met him at the auction of the Raraflora Conifer Collection near Feasterville, Pennsylvania. Raraflora was the plant collection of Fred Bergman. After he passed away, the collection and property were sold to a group of investors who proceeded to sell the plants and develop the property. Brooks was the plant expert who worked with the auctioneer.

One of the plants sold became famous throughout the nation as the most expensive plant ever bought at an auction up to that time. The original *Pinus parviflora* 'Bergman' sold for over $10,000.00, and the buyer had to pay to have it dug. It was a surprising amount of money for a plant. I had attended the auction but left after the fifth plant was sold. The selling prices were out of my financial range. Raraflora was a world famous collection, and the buyers were bidding accordingly.

Chamaecyparis obtusa 'Bess'

Chamaecyparis obtusa 'Bess' was named for a special person. Elizabeth Reis, affectionately called Bess by Joe and all who knew her, was married to Joe for many years and took great care of him when he became ill and passed away. Bess always made certain that I never left their home hungry. She would feed me lunch, and sometimes I stayed overnight and had supper and breakfast as well. I seldom drove home without a sack of Long Island bagels on the seat beside me, thanks to Bess.

The plant, *Chamaecyparis obtusa* 'Bess', is as special as its namesake. Joe sold me an old plant, one of the first propagations from the original seedling. It was over twenty years old and less than 2' (60 cm) tall. It is an exceptionally slow growing, densely branched selection with a narrowly conical shape. It grows about 1" (3 cm) per year. I still have the plant, and it is about fifty years old and only 6' (2 m) tall and less than 3' (1 m) wide.

Like most Hinoki cypresses, 'Bess' is propagated by rooting cuttings. It is best grown in fertile, well drained, moist soil and is a special addition to any small garden. The slow growth rate and conical shape are not an easy combination to find and make a nice contrast with the relatively abundant cushions sometimes found at specialty nurseries.

It may be difficult to locate, but *Chamaecyparis obtusa* 'Bess' is well worth the search. Joe Reis enjoyed naming plants after family members, and one of his best was named for the very special lady in his life.

During the 1920's, William Gardner collected and germinated seed from *Chamaecyparis obtusa* 'Nana Gracilis' at Red Lodge Nursery, England. Around 1930 he made a number of selections from his seedlings and introduced them into cultivation. *Chamaecyparis obtusa* 'Spiralis' was one of those seedlings.

If ever a plant was aptly named, it is *Chamaecyparis obtusa* 'Spiralis'. I list it here because it has a number of similarities to 'Bess'. This dwarf, upright, conical plant has cup-shaped, flattened sprays of foliage that twist around the smaller branchlets, creating an attractive feature that gives this plant its name. It grows about 2' (60 cm) high in thirty years while staying quite narrow. Perhaps its best use is in a garden with an oriental flavor, especially since some judicious pruning will accentuate its unique growth characteristics. Otherwise use *Chamaecyparis obtusa* 'Spiralis' in the garden in the same way as you would 'Bess'.

Private Garden

Chamaecyparis obtusa 'Bess'

Chamaecyparis obtusa 'Spiralis'
Iseli Nursery

Chamaecyparis obtusa 'Bess'
Coenosium Gardens

Chamaecyparis obtusa 'Butterball'

When I lived in the Northeast, Long Island was the part of the world where old conifer collections with many special cultivars abounded. Unfortunately they were off limits to most conifer collectors. However, there were several people who lived on the Island who had their own little estates. Even if they were the size of a quarter of a city lot, they were real treasures and the owners were very friendly. Names like Joe Reis, Eddie Rezek, Joe Burke, and Joel Spingarn spring to mind.

They were all very active with conifer seedlings with Reis, Rezek, and Spingarn mainly focusing on *Chamaecyparis obtusa* seedlings. Rezek grew a dwarf, golden one that he named 'Butterball' while Spingarn had a similar one that he named 'Golden Sprite'. Reis had some nice golden seedlings as well, but none that were dwarf.

Chamaecyparis obtusa 'Golden Sprite' is a miniature selection that is globose and dense with a slightly uneven outline. Flattened sprays arch outward from the center as it grows about ½" (1 cm) per year. The gold foliage is moderately resistant to sun scald but does need some protection. It also seems to be one of the less winter hardy selections of *Chamaecyparis obtusa*. In spite of its shortcomings, it has become very popular due to its diminutive size and bright color. It was grown as a seedling by Joel Spingarn, Long Island, New York, and introduced about 1979 in Welch's *Manual of Dwarf Conifers*.

The seedling selected about the same time by Eddie Rezek, *Chamaecyparis obtusa* 'Butterball', did not receive the publicity of 'Golden Sprite' and is just now becoming more widely popular and available. 'Butterball' is a dwarf, globose selection with bright yellow foliage. It is very resistant to sunscald and hardier than 'Golden Sprite'. The sprays do not arch horizontally outward like those of 'Golden Sprite'. They are more typical to the species by maintaining a vertical habit. The branching is not quite as dense as that of 'Golden Sprite', which allows better air circulation with less chance of disease problems that sometimes attack 'Golden Sprite'.

Both of these selections are choice additions to any garden with their small size and bright yellow foliage. The slight difference in growth habit makes them interchangeable for most uses, but 'Butterball' has a greater chance of reaching maturity.

Chamaecyparis obtusa 'Butterball'
Kools garden

Chamaecyparis obtusa 'Golden Sprite'
Linssen garden

Chamaecyparis obtusa 'Elf'

Humphrey Welch visited the United States during the early 1970's when he was working on the second edition of his dwarf conifer book for Theophrastus Press. He spent considerable time with some of the major conifer collectors of that time. One of these was Joel Spingarn on Long Island. While visiting with Spingarn, Welch was shown a group of *Chamaecyparis obtusa* seedlings Spingarn had grown from his own collected seed. Welch became very enthusiastic and convinced Spingarn to name them all so they could be introduced through his book.

Spingarn lived in a very interesting location since there were three other avid conifer collectors within a short distance: Joe Reis, Eddie Rezek, and Henry Weissenberger. The four of them were actively growing and evaluating seedlings from *Chamaecyparis obtusa* and had named a number of excellent selections. Spingarn and Welch were about to add more choice plants to this group.

A number of Spingarn's selections have not withstood the test of time. Among the better plants from this group, are 'Little Ann', 'Dainty Doll', and 'Leprechaun', with one very special plant standing out. *Chamaecyparis obtusa* 'Elf' is a miniature selection with the distinctive characteristic of developing an ellipsoid shape as it grows into a dense little bush. It grows about 1" (2 cm) per year with dense, dark green foliage. Even a grafted plant will exhibit a slow growth as demonstrated by a number of twenty-year old grafted plants in my own collection that are less than 15" (30 cm) in diameter.

The ellipsoid character of this plant makes it unique among the miniature selections of *Chamaecyparis obtusa* and creates an exceptional addition to the landscape. It is especially nice in a rock garden setting where most miniatures are flattened cushions. It does very well in full sun to partial shade in well drained, moist soils. Grafting it onto *Thuja occidentalis* for clay soils has a minor effect upon its growth rate.

Chamaecyparis obtusa 'Golden Sprite' is the other miniature selection from Spingarn's original group of seedlings. Its bright yellow color and downturned tips are unique and exciting. 'Golden Sprite' would have been more popular than 'Elf', except it suffers from sun scald, the hardiness is questionable, and it is disease prone. It is an excellent addition to the landscape if one is lucky enough to have the necessary conditions to grow it well.

Chamaecyparis obtusa 'Little Ann'
Van Kempen garden

Chamaecyparis obtusa 'Elf'
Helms garden

Chamaecyparis obtusa 'Juniperoides' and other Red Lodge seedlings

William Gardner is a name that may or may not be well known among conifer collectors, but he has had an important impact in the world of *Chamaecyparis obtusa* aficionados He was associated with W. H. Rogers & Son, Red Lodge Nursery, Chandlers Ford, Hampshire, England.

During the 1920's, Gardner was employed at Red Lodge Nursery where he collected and germinated seed from *Chamaecyparis obtusa* 'Nana Gracilis'. About 1930 he made a number of selections from his seedlings and introduced them into cultivation. *Chamaecyparis obtusa* 'Juniperoides' was one of the smallest of these selections. It is not an easy plant to locate, but it is well worth the effort.

Chamaecyparis obtusa 'Juniperoides' is a miniature, globose plant with sparsely arranged branches and fan shaped, decurving sprays of dark green foliage contributing to a rather open growth habit for such a diminutive cultivar. It will grow to about 10" (25 cm) in diameter after about thirty years. Its growth rate is about ½" (1 cm) per year. *Chamaecyparis obtusa* 'Juniperoides' can be grown in conditions ranging from full sun to partial shade. It needs good drainage as well as decent air circulation and persistent soil moisture.

Other plants from this famous group of seedlings include 'Bartley', 'Bassett', 'Caespitosa', 'Juniperoides Compacta', 'Laxa', 'Minima', 'Spiralis', 'Stoneham', and 'Verdon'. Of this group, 'Spiralis' and 'Verdon' have become very popular and are suitable for smaller to mid-sized gardens with a few caveats.

Chamaecyparis obtusa 'Caespitosa' is even slower than 'Juniperoides' with a slightly denser growth habit and the cup-shaped or shell-like foliage common within this group of seedlings. The foliage shape was inherited from 'Nana Gracilis', which has this as an identifying characteristic. 'Caespitosa' has a tufted appearance to its foliage, making it distinct from 'Juniperoides'. It can be used in the same way as 'Juniperoides'. The conifer collector may desire both plants, but the discerning gardener can use either one rather than both.

Chamaecyparis obtusa 'Juniperoides' Linssen garden

C. o. 'Laxa'
Vermeulen garden

Chamaecyparis obtusa 'Caespitosa'
Trompenburg Arboretum

Chamaecyparis obtusa 'JR'

I made many friends when I started conifer collecting. Most of them were considerably older than I was so they enjoyed helping a young person develop an interest in conifer collecting. I miss visiting with them and talking conifers. I guess I have taken their place since they are gone, and I have become a seasoned citizen. Joe Reis of Long Island, New York, was one of my good friends. He died over twenty-five years ago, but I think of him every time I look at one of his plants in my garden. Joe was one of the early experimenters with seeds from *Chamaecyparis obtusa*. I believe it was his favorite conifer species. His first selection was *Chamaecyparis obtusa* 'Reis Dwarf', a very special selection that eventually can grow quite large.

When I met Joe in the late 1970's, he had retired and was running a small nursery from his postage stamp-sized back yard. As we developed a close relationship, he parted with a few of his very special discoveries. *Chamaecyparis obtusa* 'JR' was one of these. Joe had given this seedling selection a name comprised of his two first initials. People call it Junior, but that is incorrect.

Chamaecyparis obtusa 'JR' is a miniature cushion. When Joe sold me one of his first propagations from the original plant, it was about twenty years old. A dark green selection, it grows less than 1" (.5 cm) per year. 'JR' is not easy to find, but some nurseries will have it available in smaller sizes. It requires well drained, moist soil and does very well in the full sun. It is not the only cushion-shaped Hinoki cypress, but it is arguably the best.

The 'JR' I purchased from Joe is still in my collection. It has survived several transplantings and is now happily positioned next to my hundred year-old *Chamaecyparis obtusa* 'Nana'. Meanwhile, Joe's original plant is in a private Long Island garden.

Reis garden

Reis garden

Chamaecyparis obtusa 'Mariesii'

I have always been attracted to variegated conifers so a visit to Watnong Nursery in New Jersey was especially rewarding when I came across a diminutive bun that had white speckled foliage in a small container.

Chamaecyparis obtusa 'Mariesii' is a dwarf, rounded bush that becomes conical as it ages. Occasional light pruning is needed from time to time to maintain the dense growth habit and good color. It grows about ½" (1 cm) per year with white tipped foliage that becomes yellowish-white during the winter. Since it does not burn, it can be grown in full sun or partial shade with equally good results. The white is not overpowering and adds a nice, somewhat subdued, contrast to other plants in the garden.

First listed in 1900 by Veitch, this cultivar has apparently been given other names with varying descriptions through the years ('Nana Albovariegata' and 'Nana Argentea'). Reference to its dwarfness was first noted under the name 'Nana Argentea' by Hornibrook in 1939. In American gardens this selection commonly reverts and sends out faster sprays, often with different shades of whitish foliage.

Chamaecyparis obtusa 'Mariesii' is typically grown from rooted cuttings and needs well drained, moist soil. A rock garden setting is ideal since rock gardens have well drained, moist soil and are generally planted with miniature or dwarf conifers and alpine plants.

Valley Garden

*A very old specimen at the
Hillier Arboretum*

Chamaecyparis obtusa 'Nana'

When anyone goes to a garden center and asks for a dwarf Hinoki cypress, *Chamaecyparis obtusa* 'Nana' is the plant that fits the description. More often than not, however, it is not the plant purchased. The true 'Nana' is hard to find since a myriad of other plants are offered by nurseries under this name. The most common imposter is 'Nana Gracilis' which has little in common with the much dwarfer 'Nana'.

Chamaecyparis obtusa 'Nana' is a dwarf, cushion-shaped plant that becomes broadly globose with a flattened top as it ages, eventually becoming somewhat conical. With a growth rate of about 1" (3 cm) per year, outgrowing the cushion stage takes many years.

The blackish-green foliage is shell-like and held on branchlets that are partly horizontal and partly bowed upright. Most commonly propagated from cuttings, a plant takes many years to reach a saleable size and will be available only from the most discerning nurseries. The production of 'Nana' by grafting will accelerate the growth rate and enlarge the foliage while allowing the toleration of heavier soils. Eventually a grafted plant will grow at a slower rate, but its resemblance will be more closely aligned with 'Nana Gracilis' than the true 'Nana'.

Even though it was introduced into Europe about 1861 from Japan by Dr. von Siebold, it has never been widely grown due to its slow growth rate and resultant high production cost. In the United States the largest producer of *Chamaecyparis obtusa* 'Nana' was Mitsch Nursery, Aurora, Oregon. John Mitsch purchased a mature mother plant out of California in the 1950's and used it to provide material for his nursery production. This original plant is now located in our garden and is easily 100 years old. It was the source of most of the plants of this cultivar grown in North America.

(Continued)

Chamaecyparis obtusa 'Nana'
Helms garden

Chamaecyparis obtusa 'Hage'
Trompenburg Arboretum

Chamaecyparis obtusa 'Nana' (cont.)

We purchased this *Chamaecyparis obtusa* 'Nana' from Mitsch Nursery in 2007. When moved from Oregon to Eatonville, Washington, the tree was hand dug: the 5000 pound (2100 kg) burlap ball was tightly laced and transported on a heavy equipment trailer. When I removed approximately one third of the foliage upon planting, the plant did not even go off color through the first summer in its new home. It is 9' (3 m) tall by 5' (1.7 m) wide with a massive internal branch structure and creates a centerpiece to our gardens.

A dwarf, dense, broadly conical selection with twisted, crowded branches, *Chamaecyparis obtusa* 'Hage' grows to about 3' (1 m) in twenty years. Its foliage is dark green with small needles. Originating about 1928 at the William Hage and Co. Nursery, Boskoop, Holland, it is easily confused with 'Nana' when it is young. However, *Chamaecyparis obtusa* 'Nana' is a slower growing plant, and the foliage is more minute and cup-shaped than that of 'Hage'.

Either of these selections will work very nicely wherever a small, dark green, conical plant is wanted in the landscape. With their slow growth rates, they are interchangeable and especially valued in the smaller oriental themed garden. They both prefer full sun but will do very well in partial shade. Heavy shade will result in a more open growth habit.

Chamaecyparis obtusa 'Nana' ready to move to Coenosium Gardens

Chamaecyparis obtusa 'Hage'
Coenosium Gardens

Chamaecyparis obtusa 'Nana' in its new home at Coenosium Gardens

Chamaecyparis obtusa 'Nana Gracilis'

When purchasing a dwarf Hinoki cypress, the scientific name becomes very important because using just a descriptive name is a recipe for problems since many different selections fit that description. Perhaps the most commonly sold plant under this name is *Chamaecyparis obtusa* 'Nana Gracilis'. It is a dense-growing, dwarf, pyramidal bush with a rugged, picturesque outline. It is not as dwarf as sales people sometimes say. It grows to 10' (3 m) in height with a width of up to 6' (2 m) after about twenty-five years.

If the gardener is prepared for the eventual size of 'Nana Gracilis', it can be used as a focal point or a great accent for the moderately sized garden. The foliage is dark green on branchlets that take on a characteristic shell-form shape, and it will thrive in full sun or partial shade.

When 'Nana Gracilis' is propagated by grafting, it will grow at an accelerated rate for the first ten years before assuming a more typical rate of less than 6" (15 cm) per year. The most common understock used, *Thuja occidentalis*, allows this species to be grown in heavier soils. If it is grown on its own roots, it must have well drained, moist soil. In Boskoop, Holland, grafting is the preferred method of propagation since most of the nurseries must sell their plants within two years so a faster rate of growth is needed.

Chamaecyparis obtusa 'Nana Gracilis' was introduced before 1891 and has proven to be a source of many new selections. These selections originated as seedlings grown from 'Nana Gracilis' and show a wide range of growth rates from miniature through almost species normal. I have described a number of these seedlings in this book.

Hillier Arboretum

Chamaecyparis obtusa 'Nana Lutea'

Some people think that a conifer with golden foliage is sick and dying. Although it is true that sick conifers often turn yellow before dying, the shade of yellow they assume is obviously an unhealthy one. Conifers selected for their golden hue have a healthy depth to their color, and a number of healthy variations glow in the garden. *Chamaecyparis obtusa* 'Nana Lutea' is an early selection of golden Hinoki cypress that is very popular, but not very easy to locate, especially in larger sizes.

Originating as a sport on *Chamaecyparis obtusa* 'Nana Gracilis', it was introduced in Europe in 1966 by Jan Spek, Boskoop, Holland. *Chamaecyparis obtusa* 'Nana Lutea' is a dwarf, compact, conical bush that grows slightly faster than 'Nana'. Its foliage is clear, pale-yellow that will burn in the sun on younger plants. As it ages and shades more of its own interior, the sun scald becomes less of an issue and the brightness reaches its full intensity.

Chamaecyparis obtusa 'Nana Lutea' is an excellent companion plant to *Chamaecyparis obtusa* 'Nana Gracilis', and if planted together in groups of three, they will make a statement in any landscape. Grow it in the full sun, but give it some sun protection until it is about 3' (1 m) tall.

Chamaecyparis obtusa 'Verdon' has a number of similarities and advantages over *Chamaecyparis obtusa* 'Nana Lutea'. It is easier to locate and purchase and will not burn in the full sun. Its bright gold foliage is not quite as bright as 'Nana Lutea' but will be more than suitable in the typical garden setting. The growth rate of 'Verdon' is slightly faster than 'Nana Lutea', but the shape, fullness, and size after twenty years are all within acceptable parameters to make it an acceptable alternative. Some winter bronzing of 'Verdon' is one of the most obvious differences between the two selections.

(continued)

Chamaecyparis obtusa 'Nana Lutea'
Mitsch Nursery

Chamaecyparis obtusa 'Verdon'
Mitsch Nursery

Chamaecyparis obtusa 'Nana Lutea' (cont.)

Chamaecyparis obtusa 'Verdon' originated as one of a group of seedlings from 'Nana Gracilis', which was collected and grown by George Gardner, nursery foreman at the Red Lodge Nursery, Chandlers Ford, Hampshire, England. This group of seedlings provided an extensive number of dwarf cultivars since 1923 (Hornibrook) to the present as old plants occasionally surface.

Use *Chamaecyparis obtusa* 'Verdon' in the same way as *Chamaecyparis obtusa* 'Nana Lutea' with the knowledge that it will tolerate greater exposure to the sun and will have more flexibility of use.

Chamaecyparis obtusa
'Nana Lutea'
Hachman Nursery

Chamaecyparis obtusa 'Verdon'
Mitsch Nursery

Chamaecyparis obtusa 'Snowkist'

Gordon Bentham, a retired butcher who lived in Victoria, British Columbia, was an avid conifer collector and very generous with his plants. One of his close friends was William Goddard, owner of Floravista Gardens, also in Victoria. Goddard discovered a number of conifer sports and mutations that he introduced to cultivation. Bentham would actively distribute these new introductions to his friends. In fact, Bentham introduced himself to me by sending me a box of plants when I lived in Pennsylvania. One of these plants was my original *Picea sitchensis* 'Bentham's Sunlight' a.k.a. The Golden Spruce.

Chamaecyparis obtusa 'Snowkist' was Goddard's discovery, and Bentham was instrumental in distributing it south of the Canadian border. Discovered as a sport on 'Tonia', it possesses more of the white variegation and exhibits a slower growth rate. Like 'Tonia' the full sun increases the extent of the variegation.

Chamaecyparis obtusa 'Tonia' is a dwarf plant with a growth habit similar to 'Nana Gracilis', which is not surprising, since it originated as a sport of that cultivar. It grows slower than 'Nana Gracilis' due to its foliage: dark green with areas of white variegation mainly at the ends of the foliage sprays. 'Tonia' originated about 1928 as a sport from 'Nana Gracilis' at William Hage & Co. Nursery, Boskoop, Holland.

Use *Chamaecyparis obtusa* 'Snowkist' in the full sun with well drained, moist soil. It is fine for the rock garden but can also be used in other garden areas since it is a dwarf selection rather than miniature. The splashes of white variegation add greatly to this plant's interest.

Chamaecyparis obtusa 'Snowkist'
private garden

Chamaecyparis obtusa 'Tonia'
Van Kempen garden

Chamaecyparis obtusa 'Sparkles'

In 1992 I spent a week travelling around New South Wales in Australia with several conifer collectors: Leo Koelwyn, Ron Radford, and Don Teese. I was gathering information about the Australian conifer discoveries and visited a number of nurseries throughout the region surrounding Melbourne. Radford is from Tasmania and shared a wealth of knowledge about their conifers.

Radford had made an interesting discovery when he found a gold spot on a mature *Chamaecyparis obtusa* 'Pygmaea'. He rooted a cutting of the sport, and it proved to be a stable variegation. This fact was a bit surprising since he had discovered variegated spots on *Chamaecyparis obtusa* many times before, but they always disappeared after propagation. His persistence paid a nice dividend with *Chamaecyparis obtusa* 'Sparkles'.

Chamaecyparis obtusa 'Sparkles' is a dwarf, dense selection that grows broader than high at a rate of about 3" (7 cm) per year. Its foliage is gold and green consistently throughout the plant with no signs of reverting. It was introduced about 1990 by Radford in Tasmania after he discovered it as a small yellow spot on a 4' (1.5 m) wide plant of 'Pygmaea'. 'Sparkles' is a typical 'Pygmaea' with variegated foliage, making it a nice addition to the garden.

Use it in the full sun where a dwarf, spreading shrub with colorful foliage can add the most impact. It also responds very well to an occasional pruning if some shaping is desired.

Koeman garden

Coenosium Gardens

The *Chamaecyparis pisifera* 'Compacta' group of William Goddard

Chamaecyparis pisifera 'Compacta' is easily confused with *Chamaecyparis pisifera* 'Nana'. *Chamaecyparis pisifera* 'Compacta' is a compact, dwarf selection that becomes much wider than high with densely arranged branchlets and strong, upright-growing shoots that develop tightly packed foliage during the second year. *Chamaecyparis pisifera* 'Nana' is a dwarf, globose, cushion-shaped bun with spreading branches and very dense, fan-shaped branches. The major difference between the two is the development of the strong shoots common to 'Compacta'.

Discovered as a sport on 'Compacta' by William Goddard, Floravista Gardens, Victoria, British Columbia, about 1964, *Chamaecyparis pisifera* 'Minima Aurea' is a dwarf, cushion shaped selection with a broadly rounded top and dense foliage. It produces occasional loose sprays of foliage common to 'Compacta'. Growing about 1" (2 cm) per year, it has green foliage with a nice overall golden gleam.

During the early 1970's, Goddard introduced two sports from 'Minima Aurea'. *Chamaecyparis pisifera* 'Gold Dust' was one. It is a dwarf, cushion shaped plant with a broadly rounded top that produces occasional loose sprays of foliage and grows about 1" (3 cm) per year. Its foliage is green with patches of golden yellow variegation throughout. The other sport is *Chamaecyparis pisifera* 'Silver Lode'. Its description is the same as 'Gold Dust', with one difference: its foliage is green with patches of golden white variegation throughout.

These two sports of *Chamaecyparis pisifera* 'Minima Aurea' have similarities to *Chamaecyparis pisifera* 'Nana Albovariegata' and *Chamaecyparis pisifera* 'Compacta Variegata' in their variegations, but Goddard's plants are tidier, and the variegation is both more extensive and reliable.

Use all three of Goddard's plants in the full sun for dense, colorful mounds that will slowly spread horizontally while gaining very little vertical character. Well drained soil and good air circulation are needed. The soil needs the ability to retain some moisture as well.

Chamaecyparis pisifera 'Gold Dust'
Coenosium Garden

Chamaecyparis pisifera
'Gold Dust' foliage
Coenosium Gardens

Left is *Chamaecyparis pisifera* 'Silver Lode' foliage
Coenosium Gardens

Cryptomeria japonica 'Kilmacurragh'

I have seen a number of large specimens of *Cryptomeria japonica* 'Cristata' in various gardens throughout the United States and Europe. It has always fascinated me with its large masses of cristate foliage that take on the appearance of large cockscombs. My good friend, Joe Reis, from Merrick, New York, had an especially large specimen that produced massive cockscombs. From time to time Joe would remove one for a friend who was doing flower arrangements for a competition. It invariably led to an award winning display. Unfortunately, I knew that *Cryptomeria* would not do very well in our Pennsylvania location and despaired of ever having one in my collection.

When Dianne and I eventually purchased Mitsch Nursery in Aurora, Oregon, we became owners of a *Cryptomeria japonica* 'Cristata' that was about 50' (16 meters) tall. The large cockscombs were all near the top. The only way to enjoy them was to remove them from the tree.

Edsal Wood's Bonsai Village Nursery was only a few miles away. One of his interests was *Cryptomeria*, and he had a fairly complete collection of cultivars. One day he showed me a dwarf *Cryptomeria* with fasciated foliage (cockscombs). It was a plant named *Cryptomeria japonica* 'Kilmacurragh'. Wood didn't know the origin of this cultivar, only that it was very unique and added a special touch to the smaller landscape.

Cryptomeria japonica 'Cristata' has no place in smaller gardens since it becomes a tree. *Cryptomeria japonica* 'Kilmacurragh' on the other hand fits in any size garden. It is a dwarf form with a flattened globose growth habit and dark green foliage. Nearly all of its branches have fasciated branch tips and juvenile foliage. It grows up to 4" (10 cm) per year.

Totally different from 'Cristata', the original plant is growing in Kilmacurragh, Rathdrum, County Wicklow, Ireland. It was most likely of Japanese origin, but since the Japanese name for this plant was not known, it was called *Cryptomeria japonica* 'Kilmacurragh' by Humphrey Welch.

Use *Cryptomeria japonica* 'Kilmacurragh' in the rock garden or in a plant border with good drainage. It does well in full sun although the winter sun may be a problem in colder climates. The uniqueness of the foliage will attract attention and cause comment, especially if it is planted near a high traffic areas.

Saville Garden

Boskoop Research Station

Cryptomeria japonica 'Knaptonensis'

Cryptomeria japonica 'Knaptonensis' is a cultivar of Japanese cedar that always generates great interest with visitors. I have several in shaded locations throughout our gardens, and visitors can't miss seeing them due to their bright, white foliage (with green undertones).

Shadey areas are always difficult areas to landscape with colorful plants. However, *Cryptomeria japonica* 'Knaptonensis' is a plant that benefits from shade and does best with just a few hours of morning sunlight. It is a dwarf form with an irregularly globose outline. The branches are short and abundant, creating a very dense plant. The foliage is mostly glossy white at first, losing the gloss but retaining the white throughout the year. It will grow up to about 2" (5 cm) per year, making it very useful for smaller gardens.

Found by Hornibrook in 1930 on Madre Island, in Lake Maggiore, Italy, it was a witches' broom on 'Nana Albospica'. When describing it in his book, *Dwarf and Slow Growing Conifers*, Hornibrook explained how he took tiny cuttings from the original broom in 1922 and rooted them. Then by 1930 he lost track of all but three of the little plants. Two of those three were subsequently lost as well and the only remaining plant was one he gave to a friend by the name of Lyttel. That plant was propagated, and 'Knaptonensis' was not lost to cultivation.

It is not uncommon to find 'Knaptonensis' reverting back to the form of 'Nana Albospica' with its longer branches. The reversions are easily removed to maintain the small size of 'Knaptonensis' and extend its useful life span in the smaller garden.

Cryptomeria japonica 'Nana Albospica'
Stanley & Sons Nursery

Cryptomeria japonica 'Knaptonensis'
Coenosium Gardens

Cryptomeria japonica 'Nana Albospica'

Cryptomeria japonica 'Ryoku Gyoku'

Cryptomeria japonica, commonly called the Japanese cedar, has a number of cultivars that are considered dwarf to miniature. Most of them tend to produce coarser growing shoots that periodically need to be removed, a problem common to 'Tansu' and 'Vilmoriniana', or they have hardiness problems like 'Tenzan', a dense little globe that will survive a hard winter and then die after a subsequently moderate one.

Cryptomeria japonica 'Ryoku Gyoku' appears to be a good choice to avoid such problems. It is a densely branched globe with light green foliage and nodding branch tips. With a growth rate of less than 1" (3 cm) per year, it deserves a home in smaller gardens located in more moderate climates.

Cryptomeria japonica 'Ryoku Gyoku' was discovered by Edsal Wood at his Bonsai Village Nursery, Wilsonville, Oregon. Wood grew thousands of conifer seedlings for resale and became interested in keeping the odd ones to grow on and study for desireable attributes. He was always on the look out for naturally dwarf seedlings that he could use for bonsai plants. His interests also led him to amass a large collection of *Cryptomeria japonica* cultivars, which he propagated from cuttings to sell as bonsai plants.

Wood was good at encouraging plant cuttings to develop roots and marketed a rooting compound he produced called Wood's Rooting Hormone. The first formulations used DMSO as a penetrant to get the active ingredients (rooting hormones) through the bark into the cambium of the cutting. Later he changed to other penetrants as DMSO was proven to be unsafe for that use.

Wood became a good friend and would often visit our Canby, Oregon, nursery to purchase overgrown specimens of *Picea abies* 'Nidiformis' and 'Little Gem'. He would remove 75% of the branches and foliage from a plant, bare root it, plant it in sawdust, and water it with a dilute solution of Wood's Rooting Hormone. These plants made excellent bonsai specimens after repotting.

It was during one of my visits to Bonsai Village Nursery about 1990 that he showed me a *Cryptomeria japonica* 'Tansu' with a small, green ball at the end of one of its branches, a miniature witches' broom. He planned to root cuttings from it, and since it looked like a little green gem stone, he named it Cryptomeria japonica 'Ryoku Gyoku'.

Although *Cryptomeria japonica* 'Ryoku Gyoku' is not commonly found in garden centers, it can be located at specialty nurseries. It can be grown under conditions ranging from mostly to partially sunny with protection from the winter sun. The soils need to be well drained, a condition usually attained by planting on a berm or in a rock garden.

Coenosium Gardens

Coenosium Gardens

Cryptomeria japonica: The Two Little T's

Cryptomeria japonica 'Tenzan' is possibly the most dwarf selection of Japanese cedar available for garden use. This small green cushion grows less than 1" (2 cm) per year. It has many uses in the smaller garden but is subject to a few concerns. 'Tenzan' will easily sunscald on hot summer days. It is also more susceptible to cold damage in the winter than is typical for *Cryptomeria japonica*.

Remove any coarse foliage or shoots that appear since they are not uncommon and will eventually destroy the dwarf character of the plant. When it is kept small, it is a nice addition to a rock garden or planter or trough garden.

Growing up to about 3" (7 cm) per year, *Cryptomeria japonica* 'Tansu' has an irregular shape as it slowly grows into a broad pyramid. Its congested, green foliage becomes bronze in the winter.

Plant 'Tansu' in a rock garden or even a garden with an oriental flavor where a broad, low pyramid can add character. It even has an additional feature of growing at an angle as if it were windswept.

Use 'Tenzan' and 'Tansu' in full sun in well drained soils for the best results. Do not allow the soil to become excessively dry on a hot, sunny day or sun scald may occur. The cultivar 'Tenzan' is more susceptible to scald than is 'Tansu'.

'Tansu' at Coenosium Gardens

'Tenzan' at Vermeulen garden

Picea abies 'Brno'

The German plantsman, Gunter Horstmann, introduced many plants during his lifetime. Many of these plants were true miniatures. Some he found as seedlings or witches' brooms while others he obtained from collectors in other parts of Europe. One plant he introduced under the name of *Picea abies* 'Hasin' is almost indistinguishable from another plant that originated in the Czech Republic named *Picea abies* 'Brno'. It is possible, but unlikely, that these are the same plant introduced at two different times.

Picea abies 'Brno' originated at Brno Botanic Garden, Czech Republic, as a witches' broom on 'Barryi'. It was found by Karel Kalous in 1980 and introduced by Kalous Nursery, Poplz, Czech Republic. The only information available on 'Hasin' is that it was introduced by Horstmann. Since they are almost indistinguishable, the following information applies to both of the selections.

Picea abies 'Brno' is a dense, miniature globe with a flattened top. It grows less than 1" (1.5 cm) per year and may be the size of a soccer ball in twenty-five years. Its foliage is light green with short needles, and the winter buds are prominently displayed, producing a very attractive little conifer for every season of the year.

Plant 'Brno' where it is protected from the hot summer sun. I have seen 'Brno' suffer from sun scald during a summer hot spell, especially if the ground is dry. This problem is not uncommon with most of the densely branched, miniature forms of *Picea abies*. If it is used in a rock garden in the full sun, put 'Brno' on the north side of a large rock for protection. This little prize will never outgrow its location in the smallest garden.

Beran garden - 'Brno' on left

Coenosium Gardens

Coenosium Gardens

Picea abies 'Clanbrassiliana'

I have always been as interested in the history of conifer cultivars and the people who found and introduced them as I have been in the plants themselves. *Picea abies* 'Clanbrassiliana' found its way into my collection in the 1970's. A wholesale nursery in New Jersey had an assortment of overgrown *Picea abies* available, and *Picea abies* 'Clanbrassiliana' was on the list. The plant I bought was terribly root bound but survived my "slash and tear" planting technique. It was the typical North American form of this cultivar: a dense, mounding bush that grew about 3" (8 cm) per year. I believed my collection now had a specimen of the first dwarf conifer ever named. *Picea abies* 'Clanbrassiliana' was found about 1780 or earlier on the Moira Estate, near Belfast, Ireland, and Lord Clanbrassil brought it to his country residence, Tolleymore in County Down, where the original plant is still growing.

In the mid 1980's, I was visiting public and private gardens in Holland with my very good friend, Dick van Hoey Smith. We spent a day at the Gimborn Pinetum touring the conifer collection. Next to the main path was a specimen of *Picea abies* that was about 8' (3 m) high and looked like a giant, old style honeybee hive. It was a specimen of *Picea abies* 'Clanbrassiliana' that was over one hundred years old. It was nothing like the plant I had in my garden under that name. Upon closer examination I noticed some faster growth at its base that matched the plant in my garden. That was when I discovered that my *Picea abies* 'Clanbrassiliana' was reverted growth and not the true form. Shortly thereafter I was able to obtain scion wood that I could trace back to the Gimborn specimen. Plants from these scions are now growing here at Coenosium Gardens.

Picea abies 'Clanbrassiliana' is a dwarf form with a habit more or less "beehive"-shaped. The branches are thin and flexible with an annual growth rate of about 1" (3 cm). Young plants are narrowly conical and very densely branched. 'Clanbrassiliana' is commonly propagated by grafting but will also root from cuttings. Interestingly enough, plants seem truer to form when grafted rather than rooted.

Plant it in full sun to maintain its compactness, and remove any coarse, faster growth that may appear to prevent this growth from dominating.

Gimborn Pinetum

Coenosium Gardens

Picea abies 'Dumpy'

Great Britain has many world famous gardens. I have toured a number of these as well as several private gardens belonging to a number of my conifer friends. Near Winchester, England, is the Hillier Arboretum with its world famous dwarf conifer collection. This collection is old enough that some of the dwarf conifers provide shade from the afternoon sun for visitors. Lady Barbara Hillier was a most gracious person and lived there for many years after Sir Harold died. Dianne and I and our friend Derek Dibben, a conifer collector from Winchester, spent a day at the arboretum. When I went to the main house and tapped on the living room window to get Lady Barbara's attention, Derek expected to get arrested and banned from the gardens for life. He was not aware that she was expecting us. After a nice tea, we spent the rest of the day at Derek's garden in Winchester.

Derek had a very unique garden. Due to limited space, he kept many of his conifers in containers. That way he could move the containers around as the plants aged. Among the conifers he showed us were some very nice selections that deserved to be more readily available to gardeners everywhere. One of these plants was *Picea abies* 'Dumpy'.

Picea abies 'Dumpy' originated from a witches' broom on a dwarf form of *Picea abies* called 'Pygmaea'. 'Dumpy' grows less than 1" (3 cm) per year and develops into a dense little egg-shaped plant with dark green foliage. It will scorch on a hot summer day in the full sun, a problem with most of the miniature forms of *Picea abies*. It would benefit from mid-afternoon shade in most climates.

Picea abies 'Dumpy' is one of those plants that exhibits a faster growth rate when it is grafted. When it is grown on its own roots from a cutting, the growth rate is less than ½" (1 cm). I believe Derek's plant was on its own roots. He told me it was almost twenty years old, and I could see it was smaller than a soccer ball. I have several grafted as well as a few rooted 'Dumpy's in our gardens. The rooted ones are growing much slower than the grafted plants. However, as the grafted plants age, their growth rates slow. Eventually they will be indistinguishable from each other except that the grafted plants will be the size of fifty-year-old plants when they are just twenty years old.

Use *Picea abies* 'Dumpy' in the landscape wherever a dense, small, oval bush is desired. It will never outgrow its spot in almost any garden. The number of *Picea abies* cultivars is intimidating, and more are added every day. This one, however, stands out from "the pack".

Coenosium Gardens

Beran garden

Picea abies 'Ellwangeriana'

In 1985 Dianne and I made a decision to move to Oregon where I would join my good friend, Jean Iseli, as Vice-President in charge of plant development at Iseli Nursery. It meant leaving our Pennsylvania family and friends to "follow the Oregon Trail". I had been very active in maintaining a number of close relationships among east coast conifer collectors. I had developed an especially close relationship with Layne Ziegenfuss of Hillside Gardens Nursery ever since I first met him in 1975. He was one of the top conifer experts in the country and lived ten minutes from our Pennsylvania home.

At the time we were planning our move of household furnishings and approximately ten thousand plants (in two semis), I became aware that Layne needed another car and was short of cash. Dianne had a 1973 Buick Electra in excellent condition that we had decided to sell. Layne had several older stock plants that I liked, so I made him a deal: one Buick Electra for five of his older stock plants.

Picea abies 'Ellwangeriana' was one of these stock plants. He had a pair of them, one of which was on its own roots and one that had been grafted. Both were propagated at the same time as part of an experiment. The grafted plant grew about twice as fast as the rooted one, and after twenty years it was 6' (3m) tall while the plant on its own roots was about 3' (1 m) tall. I swapped for the smaller of the two plants.

Originating before 1890 in Highland Park, Rochester, New York, this selection is described as a dwarf form with a broad habit having ascending branches without a central leader and thick and stiff branches. It is also recommended that any coarse growth be removed as soon as it appears.

I have discovered that the coarse growth is relative to its growth rate and is most noticeable on grafted specimens of 'Ellwangeriana'. This is one of those cultivars of *Picea abies* that shows accelerated growth when it is grafted and slower growth when it is grown from a cutting. It tends to be narrow and adds a vertical element to the smaller garden, even when produced by grafting. Plant it in sunny locations where its assymetrical outline can contribute to the aesthetics of the garden. This cultivar is not easy to find, especially on its own roots, but is worth the search.

The upper plant to the right is a ten year old grafted plant at Coenosium Gardens while the plant below it is from a rooted cutting and almost thirty years old. It is the plant I traded the Buick to obtain and was growing at Mitsch Nursery when I took the picture in 1989.

Picea abies 'Formanek'

The Czech Republic is a very busy place in the world of conifers. For a number of years Czech conifer collectors have been actively collecting and propagating witches' brooms. I have visited with a number of these collectors several times and discovered that one of the best *Picea abies* selections was made years before any of them were born.

In 1906 a prostrate seedling was selected by a man named Formanek, who put his name on it. Planted at the Pruhonice Arboretum near Prague, Czech Republic, the original plant is still doing very well on a hillside next to the main path.

In 1992 I visited the Pruhonice Arboretum with two good Czech friends. We were there so I could see the most famous plant in their country, *Pinus heldreichii* 'Smidtii'. As we walked along the main path, we stopped at a prostrate *Picea abies* growing down a steep slope. It was the original plant of *Picea abies* 'Formanek'.

A slow growing, prostrate selection that grows about 4" (10 cm) per year, *Picea abies* 'Formanek' is very densely branched and will tend to mound up slightly in the center as it ages. Its foliage is dark green and shows no tendency to burn in the full sun nor to suffer tip blight where it is in contact with the soil.

Use this plant to create a slow growing mat over or around rocks in full sun where the rock garden has a slope. My oldest plant is about 5' (1.7 m) wide in fifteen years.

Another prostrate selection that is easier to find, *Picea abies* 'Frohburg' will grow about 6" (15 cm) per year while also maintaining a completely prostrate growth habit. The plant pictured here is growing down a slope behind *Picea abies* 'Malena' at Coenosium Gardens

Staked plant at Iseli Nursery

Original plant at Pruhonice Arboretum

Picea abies 'Hildburghausen'

Only a few conifers develop into near perfect globes as they grow. *Picea abies* 'Hildburghausen' is one of them. It is a dense, perfectly shaped globe that grows up to 3" (6 cm) per year. Its light green needles stick straight out from the stems. It was first listed by G. Bohme, Germany, about 1990.

It is uncanny that a spruce can develop into a perfect globe everytime. Upon close examination I found out why it exhibits this growth pattern. Every terminal shoot grows the same length each year and produces five lateral buds.

Picea glauca 'Little Globe' is another spruce that becomes a near perfect globe. It is very dense and has a slow growth rate of just over 1" (3 cm) per year. Its foliage is slightly bicolored green and gray with needles that are not especially short. The relatively large, round, brown buds make this selection easy to identify. Discovered in 1959 as a witches' broom at the Waterford Works, Wayne, New Jersey, it was introduced by Verkade Nursery of the same location in 1968.

John Verkade was an avid plantsman and was responsible for many new conifer introductions. Verkade was especially fond of *Tsuga canadensis* and named a number of unique plants for family members. Verkade's name is familiar to anyone with knowledge of the American nursery industry. He and Jean Iseli had a friendly rivalry over new introductions, especially after Verkade introduced *Picea orientalis* 'Tom Thumb Gold'.

Both of these selections can be used in a moderately sized rock garden or as part of a garden border. They do well in full sun but may scald on a hot summer day if allowed to become too dry.

Picea glauca 'Little Globe'
Heartland Collection

Picea abies 'Hildburghausen'
Coenosium Gardens

Picea abies 'Humilis' and 'Wichtel'

Around since 1891, *Picea abies* 'Humilis' was one of the strangest selections of *Picea abies*. In the Northwest it is dwarf and narrowly conical with an irregular outline. In other parts of the world it tends to be broader and more bushlike. I first saw this plant at Hillside Gardens in Lehighton, Pennsylvania, in the collection of my friend, Layne Ziegenfuss. He told me it was often mislabeled as *Picea abies* 'Pygmaea' even though it was easy to distinguish from 'Pygmaea' due to its unique characteristic of developing three different types of foliage as it grew.

Picea abies 'Humilis' has branches that grow up to 6" (15 cm) per year. These provide open areas in a typical specimen. Other regions of the plant will grow at half that rate and have clumps of buds develop at or near the ends of the shoots. The third foliage type consists of clusters of very short branches that look like witches' brooms scattered around the plant. These growth regions are inconsistent and can vary from year to year, making for a dwarf plant with considerable interest.

In the Hillier Arboretum near Winchester, England, there is an old specimen of *Picea abies* 'Humilis'. One area of congested growth not only never changed but was tighter than normal. When the small branchlets of this area were propagated, the plants that resulted consistently grew into tiny buns without any reversions to faster growth. Evidently this was a *Picea abies* 'Humilis' with an actual witches' broom.

Gunter Horstmann was probably the first plantsman to recognize this fact and introduced propagations from this broom as *Picea abies* 'Wichtel'. At a glance, an old specimen of this cultivar may be mistaken for a moss covered rock. The annual growth rate is so slow that scion wood can only be obtained from young specimens growing in considerable shade. I cannot think of a slower growing conifer. My two oldest plants were twenty years old and about 6" (15 cm) wide and less than that high when they died. One was growing where it was exposed to the afternoon sun and scalded very badly while the other was in too much shade and apparently developed a mold problem.

Picea abies 'Wichtel' is an excellent choice for any size rock garden or even a trough garden. Remember to give it some afternoon shade, or the August sun may burn the center of the plant. *Picea abies* 'Humilis' also has a home in the smaller rock garden but is best used in a larger setting. There is even a selection of 'Humilis' found under the names of 'CLU Berry Fast' and 'CLU Berry Slow'.

The 'Wichtel' broom at
Hillier Arboretum

'Humilis' in the garden of Milan Halada

Picea abies 'Little Gem'

Possibly the most readily available and truly dwarf conifer in North America, *Picea abies* 'Little Gem', is not only well behaved, but is also easy to propagate and grow. Container nurseries in the northwestern United States can take a rooted cutting and grow it to a saleable size in two years. Extensive fertilization coupled with consistent watering will force continuous growth through the summer. Larger cuttings are obtained by using grafted standards for stock plants. The process of grafting plus using large understocks accelerate the growth rate and produce cuttings that are up to three times the normal length. As soon as they are rooted, the cuttings resume the expected growth rate for this cultivar.

My first experience with *Picea abies* 'Little Gem' occurred in the early days of Coenosium Gardens when I ordered some liners from Mitsch Nursery in Oregon. They were transplants and when they arrived, each plant looked like a golf ball. After I potted them, they maintained this somewhat spherical shape. In the seventies it was a rare conifer. Today 'Little Gem' has become fairly common.

Picea abies 'Little Gem' originated as a congested area, called a witches' broom, on *Picea abies* 'Nidiformis' at the F.J. Grootendorst Nursery in Boskoop, Holland, sometime before 1960. It had an irregularly oblately spherical shape with thin, congested twigs throughout the plant. Since the twigs exposed to the light are completely covered with small, thin needles, it has an exceptionally dense coverage of foliage. The growth rate of about 1" (3 cm) per year is dependable and results in a plant that stays reliably dwarf.

Full sun to partial shade works well for *Picea abies* 'Little Gem', but old plants will sometimes suffer sun scorch on exceptionally hot, sunny days. Well drained, moist soils will produce healthy specimens for the rock garden or other garden spots where it is not crowded by perennials. It also does well in trough gardens or other types of planters. 'Little Gem' behaves itself when grafted on a standard. Standards aren't for everybody, but they do allow *Picea abies* 'Little Gem' to be grown among perennials and other types of flowers because the plant is held above the competition and the stem is hardly visible.

An old specimen at South Seattle Community College planted in front of a *Picea abies* 'Reflexa'

Picea abies 'Malena'

My long time friend Larry Stanley and I have been swapping conifers and stories for over twenty years. In fact, before he became a good friend, he was one of our earliest customers from our days in Pennsylvania. He has photographed many conifers in our collection and he does have a favorite: *Picea abies* 'Malena'. However, I don't think it is his favorite conifer. It is just perfectly sited and always appears to be in excellent condition for a photograph.

We have a small rock garden immediately behind our house on a bank that was cut by heavy equipment when our homesite was prepared. I established the rock garden on the bank and did nothing to prepare the exposed subsoil. Its plants are growing nicely in the unprepared ground, and most are actually thriving. *Picea abies* 'Malena' is one of these.

Found in 1985 by A.G. Hauenstein, Rafz, Switzerland, *Picea abies* 'Malena' is a dense cushion in the landscape. It is slightly convex in outline and so dense that it feels solid to the touch. The foliage is green with needles that are longer and thicker than expected for such a slow growing plant. It grows about 1" (3 cm) per year and may be about 15" (35 cm) wide in ten years. It does very well in the full sun in well drained soils. Our oldest plant has never shown any sign of sun scald even though it is growing in the full afternoon sun at the top of a dry, west facing slope.

This selection may be used in any full sun location with well drained soil and evidently is resistant to sun scald, which is very unusual for a miniature *Picea abies* cultivar. *Picea abies* 'Malena' is an excellent addition to the smaller garden and will never outgrow its location.

Coenosium Gardens

Coenosium Gardens

Coenosium Gardens

Picea abies 'Nidiformis'

We built a new house in 1974, and I was anxious to landscape it with some nice plants. Being a conifer novice at the time, I had little or no idea what conifer choices were available. I visited a few discount stores and found a number of plants that quickly outgrew their locations. However, I did stumble across a few truly dwarf conifers. One of these was *Picea abies* 'Nidiformis', commonly called "bird's nest spruce". It has been one of the most commonly available dwarf conifers for many years. Not only that, it is also relatively inexpensive to purchase.

I am stretching things a bit when I call *Picea abies* 'Nidiformis' a dwarf conifer. The definition of dwarf is very subjective. It is dwarf compared to the species; however, it can outgrow its location if the gardener is not careful about its siting.

Picea abies 'Nidiformis', discovered before 1904 in the Rulemann Grisson Nursery near Hamburg, Germany, was named by Beissner in 1906. It is called the "bird's nest spruce" because of its dense, broad growth with a nest-like depression at its center. Growing up to 3" (8 cm) per year, the branchlets form tight layers, creating an exceptionally dense plant. The branches grow upward at about a 50° angle but have drooping tips while the needles possess sharp, curved hooks on their undersides, quite a unique characteristic.

Since it is easy to root from cuttings and develops rather quickly into a saleable plant, it has been very popular with nurseries since its discovery. Use it in the larger rock garden or any garden setting where a spreading evergreen shrub makes the best impression. It is very hardy and relatively pest free.

A similar plant not as readily available is *Picea abies* 'Tabuliformis', which was found before 1865 in Trianon, Versailles, France. As the name implies, this dwarf selection has a wide-spreading habit, mounding as it ages, but maintaining a flat top at all times. Even as it mounds up, the distinctive layers are easy to see. They develop from the overlapping of shoots forming a dense mat of foliage that smothers the foliage beneath. The thin, flexible shoots are held at a 50° angle to the branches and demonstrate this property throughout the plant.

Although it only grows about 3" (8 cm) per year, it does build up layers of branches while developing some width and can outgrow its location if not carefully sited. My first observation of a mature specimen of *Picea abies* 'Tabuliformis' was at the Hillier Arboretum in England where I was actually able to squat under a very old plant directly behind the Hillier home.

Use this selection much as you would use *Picea abies* 'Nidiformis'. They are very much alike, but 'Tabuliformis' does grow faster.

Picea abies 'Nidiformis'
Bernheim Forest

Picea abies 'Tabuliformis'
Hillier Arboretum

Picea abies 'Pachyphylla'

Gordon Bentham lived almost three thousand miles away from me when he introduced himself in 1977. I resided in Lehighton, Pennsylvania, while his home was in Victoria, British Columbia. One spring day I came home from teaching and found a box at the garage door. In it were ten, one gallon conifers. All of them were rare and new to my collection. One of them, *Picea sitchensis* 'Aurea', now called 'Bentham's Sunlight', has become famous as The Golden Spruce of the Haida People. Another was Gordon's favorite spruce, *Picea abies* 'Pachyphylla', not as famous but very distinctive.

Bentham was a retired butcher who had an avid interest in dwarf and unusual conifers. We became very good friends and shared a number of special experiences. Bentham was also a close friend of the Goddards who owned Flora Vista Nursery in Victoria and who were responsible for introducing a number of excellent plants to the nursery trade,

Picea abies 'Pachyphylla' is a dwarf form, exceptionally slow growing, irregular and open. The branches are very short with thick, stiff twigs. The lateral buds are round and tiny with larger terminal buds being solitary. Often a branch will not have a terminal bud. When this happens, the branch will eventually shrivel and die. The needles are very thick and fleshy with the upper surface indented and the underside keeled (kidney-shaped in cross section). On occasion a longer shoot will appear, but it will eventually resume slow growth and not be a cause for concern.

In 1938 Hornibrook listed a specimen growing in Glasnevin, Dublin, Ireland, in his own collection as being one of the few known plants. Welch verified that the plant was still there in 1976 and had grown to less than 3' (1 m) in height. This selection has actually been confused in Europe with *Picea abies* 'Lombartsii', a fast growing tree with coarse foliage. I saw a block of these at a nursery that was labeled 'Pachyphylla', as if there wasn't enough confusion in the conifer world.

This unique spruce is a great choice for the informal garden. Its thick, fleshy leaves are unique as are its short, thick branches. It adds to the vertical aspect of the garden where most dwarf forms are low or spreading. Full sun and well drained soil are ideal for good growth and color.

Coenosium Gardens

Picea abies 'Pumila Nigra'

A selection of Norway spruce that has been around for a very long time and shares many of the commercial attributes of *Picea abies* 'Nidiformis' is *Picea abies* 'Pumila Nigra'. It is a dwarf spruce that is easy to grow from cuttings, responds well to fertilization and water, and does well in the landscape. Wholesale nurseries are able to produce it at low cost and market it as a dwarf conifer.

Picea abies 'Pumila Nigra', often marketed as simply *Picea abies* 'Pumila', is a dwarf form that grows broad and flat, becoming slightly convex as it ages. The height might reach slightly above 3' (1 m) on very old plants. Its twigs are brown on top and more of an orange on their bottom sides and are thin and flexible and angled upward at 50° around the margin of the plant. The dark green needles are densely arranged on the branches and feel very stiff. It grows just over 1" (3 cm) per year. Even though it was discovered and introduced sometime before 1891, it has only become popular since the 1970's. Locating it should not be very difficult.

Old specimens of 'Pumila Nigra' may be seen throughout Europe in older arboretums where they have become essential parts of their landscapes. A hundred-year-old 'Pumila Nigra' is up to 15' (5 m) wide and 4' (1.5 m) high. It should still be considered ideal for the small garden since it takes at least one hundred years to reach that size.

Picea abies 'Maxwellii' is another selection of Norway spruce that grows similar to 'Pumila Nigra' but with very different foliage. A dwarf, round cushion that mounds up toward the center, 'Maxwelli' has many short, thick shoots at the ends of its branches with thick, dark brown buds and thick, stiff, green needles as it grows about 2" (5 cm) per year. I cannot grow 'Maxwelli' in our Northwest garden as it always reverts to the 'Pseudomaxwelli' type with accelerated growth and an open branch structure. It is much better behaved in other parts of America and throughout Europe.

Both of these spruces have many uses in the landscape. Their low, spreading form and slow growth rate make them ideal for the smaller garden. The dark green foliage throughout the year makes for a nice contrast with other seasonal colors. The large plants in the pictures are very old and attest to their dwarfness.

An old specimen of
Picea abies 'Pumila Nigra' at
Blijdenstein Pinetum

Picea abies 'Pumila Nigra'
Pruhonice Botanic Garden

Picea abies 'Maxwelli' planted in 1916 at the Arnold Arboretum

Picea abies 'Pusch'

The Arnold Arboretum, Jamaica Plain, Massachussettes, has an interesting conifer collection with many of the spruce having been planted about 1900. Among these old trees is a specimen of *Picea abies* 'Acrocona'. When I first came across it in the late 1970's, I was struck by the large number of cones. I also found it interesting that the cones were on the ends of the branches. I searched quite a while before I was able to locate and purchase one for our garden.

Picea abies 'Acrocona' is not suitable for the smaller garden. I always felt that this was an unfortunate fact of life, until about 1989 when Dianne and I were visiting Jan zu Jeddeloh in Germany. He was growing a miniature form of *Picea abies* 'Acrocona', and he had hundreds of them in a small greenhouse. He explained to me that it was discovered as a witches' broom on *Picea abies* 'Acrocona'. In effect, it is a miniature 'Acrocona', making it very suitable for the smaller garden. It had been given the name of *Picea abies* 'Acrocona Nana', which was later changed to *Picea abies* 'Pusch'. It had only recently appeared in Europe, and zu Jeddeloh planned to "corner the market".

In the spring it develops red cones on most of its branch tips, making a colorful display in the garden and showing that not only herbaceous plants produce colorful 'flowers'. It develops into an irregular mound when left to its own devices and will take over twenty years to become 2' (60 cm) high by 3' (1 m) wide. The foliage is dark green, and the cones develop normally, gradually turning brown by the fall, but they never develop any size and stay quite small.

Picea abies 'Pusch' has many uses in the garden and does what a conifer should do - produce cones. Plant it in full sun with well drained soil that need not be very fertile.

Coenosium Gardens

Coenosium Gardens

Picea abies 'Tufty'

As a conifer collector, I do love growing oddities in our gardens. Many of the "weird" and unusual conifer forms are attractive in much the same way that abstract art appeals to the art fancier. Of course, a conifer that is downright ugly does not appeal to anyone. Found by J. W. Archer, Farnham, Surrey, before 1979, *Picea abies* 'Tufty' is an unusual plant that should appeal to most gardeners, especially rock gardeners.

While traveling in England, I came across an oddity that does not become a garden asset until it is at least ten years old. Derek Dibben, a close friend who lives in Winchester, England, is an avid conifer collector and maintains most of his collection in clay pots. His garden is too small to grow anything except miniatures, and even those have to be in limited numbers. By using containers, Dibben is able to rearrange his landscape as often as needed. When we were looking at his plants, he showed me an old specimen of *Picea abies* 'Tufty'.

Picea abies 'Tufty' is a slow growing, irregularly shaped bush with curved and contorted branches shooting off in all directions. Its basic shape is irregularly globose. Its light green foliage consists of thin needles of varying lengths. In fact, the needles found along the new branchlets are nothing more than stubs. What passes for full length needles are found clustered around the terminal buds near the ends of the branchlets.

Young plants are very sparse and open, in spite of the high numbers of branches and branchlets. With a growth rate of about 2" (6 cm), it takes about ten years for a specimen to show some density. The sparsity is due to the short needles, not the lack of branches.

Propagation is tricky as the thin needles are resistant to easy removal from the base of the scion and a twig can almost be mistaken for a larch, due to the paucity of foliage. Not only is *Picea abies* 'Tufty' a conversation piece in the garden, it is also quite attractive after it fills in and deserves a home in any informal planting.

Dibben garden

Bloom garden

Picea abies 'Witches' Brood'

When I lived in Pennsylvania, Watnong Nursery was always a regular stop on my plant hunting trips through New Jersey into Long Island. The owners Don and Hazel Smith were enthusiastic plantspeople. Don specialized in *Chamaecyparis obtusa* and *Tsuga canadensis*. Don was very active until the day he passed away after stacking firewood in their home. Hazel followed him just a few years later.

I used to purchase plants from the Smiths every time I visited. In fact, I often stopped on the way home and spent the last of my cash, saving fifty cents for the toll across the Delaware River. It was on one of these visits that I noticed a dwarf, globose *Picea abies* with thin needles. Don didn't want to part with it because it had been given to him by a friend, Lincoln Foster. I did manage to talk him out of it anyway. Don was always sympathetic and had trouble saying no to me. Don called it *Picea abies* 'Millstream Broom' and thought it was a witches' broom that Linc had found.

A few years later Dianne and I visited Linc and Timmy Foster at their home, Millstream, in Falls Village, Connecticut. I discussed the plant I had gotten from Don with Linc. He told me that he had been reading about Al Fordham's work at the Arnold Arboretum with seedlings from witches' brooms when he discovered a broom in a spruce that had cones. One of the seedlings he grew from it proved to be dwarf and interesting. He had planted it at Millstream and shared a rooted cutting from it with Don Smith. He was pleased that it had found a home in my collection, especially since I was preparing to offer it for sale. We also discussed putting a better name on the plant, especially since it was not a witches' broom. Linc thought about it and came up with the name *Picea abies* 'Witches' Brood'.

Picea abies 'Witches' Brood' will be globose with thin, light green needles, growing about 2" (5 cm) per year. As it ages, it develops a terminal shoot and takes on more of a broadly conical outline. As the terminal shoot grows at about 3" (8 cm) per year, the foliage takes on a dichotomy with the upper two-thirds of the plant having the thin needles spaced all around the branchlets. The bottom third of the plant has thicker, coarser needles arranged laterally along the slightly downcurved branchlets.

After twenty years, a typical specimen will be about 4' (1.3 m) tall and 3' (1 m) wide. It is very densely branched with light green foliage. It does best in the full sun with well drained soil and even thrives in nutrient poor soils.

Coenosium Gardens

Coenosium Gardens

Picea abies 'Zajecice'

Every once-in-a-while collectors come across plant names that appear to be impossible to pronounce. I added this plant to my collection in the early 1990's when a friend gave me three little pieces of scion wood. I could not say the name, but I could see that it must be a very desireable plant.

Later, during a visit to the Czech Republic, I was discussing Czech names with my good friend Jaroslav Kazbal as he took me on a tour of Prague. First, we were talking about street names in Prague. One that sticks in my mind is "The Place Where We Boil Our Enemies". There were other streets with references to blood and cutting off various appendages of one's enemies. Later, at my hotel we discussed plant names. Many of the Czech plants are named for the village where the original broom was found while others are more descriptive. For example, *Picea abies* 'Ubranky' means "by the gate" and represents the fact that the original plant is growing by the entrance gate to its discoverer's garden.

Picea abies 'Zajecice' is a dense, globose selection with thin branchlets comprising the spring flush of new growth. It grows less than 1" (2cm) per year although as it ages, it does show a tendency to produce scattered branchlets of up to 2" (5 cm) in length. These longer branchlets then produce more typical short growth the following year. *Picea abies* 'Zajecice' maintains its dense growth habit and will be less than 2' (60 cm) in diameter when it is twenty years old.

Its light green foliage has small, thin needles. The outline is irregular due to the two different rates of a typical year's growth. It originated as a witches' broom near Zajecice, Czech Republic. The name means "place with rabbits". The original village was evidently surrounded by rabbits, sort of a Czech *Watership Down*.

This is one of those rare selections of dwarf to miniature *Picea abies* that will tolerate full sun without developing sun scald. Use it in sunny locations with good drainage where space is at a premium. *Picea abies* 'Zajecice' will be difficult to find but well worth the search.

Balatka Garden

Coenosium Gardens

Picea glauca 'Burning Well'

Usually having good recall when it comes to remembering where I obtained each of the plants in my collection, I may not always remember the date, but I do usually remember who it came from. However, *Picea glauca* 'Burning Well' has me stumped. Several years ago I was taking cuttings for propagation when a gray-blue cushion with large, shiny, cinnamon brown buds caught my eye. I thought to myself, "Why didn't I notice that before?" I even had to check the name tag. It was a very attractive *Picea glauca* 'Burning Well'. It was my only specimen and I didn't know where to acquire another. I immediately cut it, and in two years I was offering it for sale.

Thanks to some timely help from Edwin Smits, a Dutch conifer collector and friend, I learned its history. Found by Joseph (Joe) Stupka in Pennsylvania on Burning Well Road, *Picea glauca* 'Burning Well' is a cushion that grows about 1" (2-3 cm) per year. Tiny gray-blue needles completely cover its small branches. The most striking feature of this plant is its winter buds. They are large and round and tinted a dark cinnamon brown. These characteristics make it a valuable addition to the smaller garden. Plant it in the full sun in a rockery or a trough garden. It likes good air circulation and well drained soils. During hot, dry spells in the summer, give it a deep watering to prevent sun scorch; otherwise, it does just fine on its own.

Recently a similar plant from the Czech Republic has appeared in some gardens. *Picea glauca* 'Palecek' is a dense, globose selection that grows about 1" (2 cm) per year. It becomes 10" (28cm) wide by 8" (20cm) high in twelve years. Its foliage is blue-green with small, stiff needles. Originating as a witches' broom, it was found in 1973 by Daniel Pesek near Kutna Hora, Czech Republic. 'Palecek' is Czech for "small thumb". Use it in the garden just like 'Burning Well'. Their colors are similar, but 'Palecek' mounds up more in the center without the pronounced winter buds.

Picea glauca 'Burning Well'
Coenosium Gardens

Picea glauca 'Palecek'
Stanley & Sons Nursery

Picea glauca 'Cecilia'

My good friend, Layne Ziegenfuss was very proud of a witches' broom that he and Greg Williams had discovered growing along the Skippack Highway near Philadelphia, Pennsylvania. This plant led to a rift between Layne and Humphrey Welch. Ziegenfuss showed the plant to Welch when he visited him to gather information on a book he was writing. Ziegenfuss was calling the plant *Picea glauca* 'Skipjack' (I think he meant 'Skippack'). Welch liked the plant but not the name.

Welch was an engineer and applied his scientific mind to precise record keeping on the origins and characteristics of cultivated conifers. He was an author of a number of books on conifers with *Manual of Dwarf Conifers* being his major accomplishment. Once he decided he didn't like a plant name, he either changed it or did not use it. For example, he did not like the name *Pseudotsuga menziesii* 'Graceful Grace' and refused to even mention it in his book.

Welch visited Joel Spingarn on Long Island after leaving Ziegenfuss. While there he discussed 'Skippack' with Spingarn (perhaps Joel had one in his garden). Welch decided to list the plant in his book as *Picea glauca* 'Cecilia' in honor of Spingarn's first wife. Ziegenfuss was not very happy, to say the least.

Picea glauca 'Cecilia' is a miniature bun with short needles arranged radially around each branchlet. It grows about 1" (3 cm) per year in the northeastern United States. In the Northwest it grows about twice that rate. Unfortunately a large wholesale nursery has been producing 'Cecilia' for over twenty years from wood originally sent to them by Ziegenfuss, and they have destroyed the plant's character. Their plants grow almost 6" (15 cm) per year. I believe they always used strong shoots for propagation which gradually destroyed its dwarfness.

Picea glauca 'Cecilia' has silvery-gray to blue foliage. Its winter buds are globular and dark brown. Use it in the mid sized rock garden in the full sun with good soil drainage. It may be found in Europe under the name 'Stanley's Pygmy'.

Koemens garden

Coenosium Gardens

Picea glauca 'Pixie': Its Siblings and Mother Plant

Among my first dwarf conifer purchases was a pair of dwarf Alberta spruces. I figured that there was no way to go wrong with a couple of miniature Christmas trees. I thought they would be perfect for our home's foundation planting. Then I met Layne Ziegenfuss.

Layne became a good friend who taught me many things about conifers and their propagation. Early on, he showed me a row of dwarf Alberta spruces his father had planted along their driveway. I had to lean backwards to see their tops. They were about 10' (3 m) tall and half that wide. I realized then that I could not always judge dwarfness by a name. *Picea glauca* 'Conica' was only dwarf in comparison to the species. It needed considerable space to develop in the landscape.

Picea glauca 'Conica' was discovered in the wild in 1904 by Alfred Rehder and J. G. Jack in the mountains near Lake Laggan, Alberta, Canada, while they were waiting for a train. They found four small plants, probably seedlings from a witches' broom of *Picea glauca*. They sent the plants to the Arnold Arboretum where they were propagated and soon found their way into the nursery industry.

The dwarf Alberta spruce is a perfect nursery plant. It is easily to root from cuttings, and it can be pushed into continuous growth as a container plant with heavy fertilization and a lot of water, making it cheap to produce. It can then be sold as a dwarf conifer with a number of valuable attributes. It is so densely branched as to appear almost solid from a short distance. The shape is a perfectly smooth pyramid with no pruning, and its light green foliage color is quite attractive.

On the other hand, there are just a couple of "minor" problems with the plant. *Picea glauca* 'Conica' will have two to three flushes of growth each season for a total length of up to about 4" (10 cm) per year. Its juvenile appearing foliage of soft, thin needles is held radially around each of its small, thin branches. Changing from a conical shape when young to a broadly conical shape when old, its major problems are red spider mite and sun scald. During hot, dry summers the red spider mite will often destroy large areas of foliage, eventually killing or badly deforming a specimen. A hot summer day, or a very bright winter day with snow on the ground, will cause sun scald on the southern side of a specimen. Careful maintenance and siting can help prevent these problems.

Picea glauca 'Conica' was mass produced from the 1930's into the 1950's and became so common that spider mites had a population explosion, and trees were decimated throughout the United States. By 1960 *Picea glauca* 'Conica' became almost a rare conifer. It was rediscovered in the 1970's, and Oregon nurseries alone were selling millions every year into garden centers around the country. Problems are more easily controlled with methods as simple as flushing the interior of a specimen with a garden hose every week or two during the summer to discourage spider mites.

(continued)

Picea glauca 'Pixie Dust'
Iseli Nursery

Picea glauca 'Pixie'
Buchholz Nursery

Picea glauca 'Pixie': Its Siblings and Mother Plant
(cont.)

Of course, the poor siting of this plant due to the misrepresentation of its mature size leads to a whole different set of problems. *Picea glauca* 'Conica' works well when it is used in a more formal garden setting provided it is given sufficient room to grow. Do not use it in smaller garden areas where a truly dwarf plant is needed. A number of selections made from mutations on *Picea glauca* 'Conica' are reliably dwarf and will not outgrow their locations.

The most dwarf selection of 'Conica' yet found is *Picea glauca* 'Pixie'. This miniature pillar is extremely dense and grows about 1" (3 cm) per year. Its light green foliage has prominent round buds. Discovered by William Goddard, Floravista Gardens, Victoria, British Columbia, about 1964, this selection is very difficult to root or to graft. It seems to root best from soft wood and to graft best onto *Picea glauca* 'Conica'. It has the same problems as 'Conica' and when grown in the full sun, it may sun-scald on its south side.

Three interesting color sports exist, two of which were found at Iseli Nursery, Boring, Oregon. *Picea glauca* 'Rainbow's End' is a typical *Picea glauca* 'Conica' in every way but one. Its second flush of growth is bright yellow, provided the days and nights are warm when the flush is occurring. Likewise, Picea glauca 'Pixie Dust' is a typical *Picea glauca* 'Pixie' in every way but one. Its second flush of growth is bright yellow, provided the days and nights are warm when it is flushing. Both of these selections look like decorated Christmas trees when this color variation occurs.

Picea glauca 'Daisey's White' is the third color variant to be discovered. It has nearly white new growth in the spring, making it a beacon in the garden. Then after several weeks of outstanding color display, it slowly turns green while retaining a white frosted appearance. It may burn slightly on an early hot, summer day so some partial afternoon shade is beneficial.

Discovered in 1979 by L. Jeurisen-Wijnen from Belgium as a mutation on *Picea glauca* 'Conica', its creamy white spring color is striking. In my garden *Picea glauca* 'Daisey's White' grows at about half the rate of 'Conica'. It also appears to be more resistant to red spider, since the foliage color may fool those pests to some extent.

Recently a witches' broom was found on a 'Daisey's White' and is being introduced as a new cultivar named *Picea glauca* 'Spring Surprise'. A dense, miniature globe covered with white tips in the spring, it will be the size of a grapefruit in five to six years.

Other forms derived from *Picea glauca* 'Conica' are appearing in conifer listings. Taking care to use the proper siting in the garden and practicing the proper pest control will ensure good experiences for the gardener.

Picea glauca 'Daisey's White'
Linssen garden

Picea glauca 'Spring Surprise'
Kohout garden

Gunter Horstmann and His Serbian Spruces

Gunter Horstmann was a true plantsman. He had a knack for finding new conifers both as seedlings and as witches' brooms. He was always willing to share his discoveries and was well known and respected throughout the "conifer world" of collectors and growers. He focused on dwarf conifers but also had several larger growing discoveries that have become very popular. Horstmann has been mentioned several times in this book for his work with the smaller growing selections.

Picea omorika has produced a number of excellent garden selections with a wide variety available from collectors and nurseries throughout Europe. Although not nearly as prolific in producing mutations as *Picea abies*, it is by no means any sort of a slacker. Horstmann found his share of *Picea omorika* witches' brooms and shared them with other collectors.

Picea omorika 'Schneverdingen' was named for Horstmann's hometown. It is a dense, little globe that grows about 1" (2 cm) per year. The bicolored foliage adds to its appeal. I have had problems maintaining it in our garden and have lost several since it seems to be prone to fungal disease. Two other selections from Horstmann have proven to be much more successful.

Picea omorika 'Gunter' was originally listed as 'Hexenbesen #1' but was later given a name in his memory. Horstmann was one of those collectors who would not use his own name for one of his discoveries. 'Gunter' is an excellent choice for the smaller garden. In twenty years it will be a globe 3' (1 m) in diameter. The branching is very dense, and it is covered by a mantle of blue, silver, and green foliage.

Elisabeth and Gunter Horstmann were married for many years, and it is only fitting that *Picea omorika* 'Gunter' should also have a mate. *Picea omorika* 'Elisabeth' was formerly known as 'Hexenbesen #3'. It needs considerable vertical space but makes a small "footprint" in the garden. Growing tall and narrow, *Picea omorika* 'Elisabeth' becomes a narrow spire. It grows about 4" (10 cm) per year, and by the time it is 10' (3 m) tall, it will be about 3' (1 m) wide. The branch structure is very dense as the branches grow laterally rather than upward as in fastigiated conifers or pendulous as in the weeping forms.

Picea omorika 'Pimoko' originated as a witches' broom in the W. Wuestemeyer Nursery, Germany, in 1980. This dwarf form grows about 2" (5 cm) per year and becomes a slightly flattened globe. It is very similar to 'Gunter' but grows slightly faster and has a slightly flattened top. Either 'Gunter' or 'Pimoko' can serve the same purpose in the smaller garden and have many similarieties.

Plant these selections in full sun and well drained soils for best results. While 'Gunter' and 'Pimoko' work well in rock gardens, 'Elisabeth' is more of a border or background plant.

'Elisabeth' to the left and 'Gunter' above at Coenosium Gardens

Picea omorika 'Peve Tijn' and its parent

I was photographing plants in Wiel Linssen's garden when I noticed a bright yellow globe. Upon closer examination I determined it was a dwarf form of *Picea omorika* with tricolored foliage - yellow on top with green and silver underneath.

Linssen kept the plant sheared so it would produce many fresh growing tips giving it a bright yellow color. If the plant is not sheared, the color is just as good but not as intense. This plant, *Picea omorika* 'Peve Tijn', is a yellow form of *Picea omorika* 'Nana'.

During a later visit to Holland, I saw the original sport at the nursery of Piet Vergeldt. In his garden a plant of *Picea omorika* 'Nana' had developed a golden area consisting of several branches. When Vergeldt propagated the branches, he observed several different growth habits and color intensities among the plants that resulted. He selected the best plant and introduced it through his nursery, naming it *Picea omorika* 'Peve Tijn' for his youngest son, Tijn.

Picea omorika 'Peve Tijn' will grow up to 4" (10 cm) per year. It is globose when young, becoming broadly conical as it ages. The full sun will intensify its color, and although it may burn slightly when young, it will outgrow that tendency as it ages. It is a bit large for the rock garden but may be used wherever a slow growing, bright yellow plant will make a statement.

Picea omorika 'Nana' is an old selection and the easiest of the dwarf Serbian spruces to locate. It was found as a witches' broom and introduced about 1930 by Goudkade Nursery, Boskoop, Holland. With a growth rate of 2" (5 cm) in most parts of America, it becomes a dense, broadly conical shrub. The branches vary in length so the outline is not perfectly symmetrical. In the northwestern United States this selection can grow up to 6" (15 cm) per year, while still maintaining its dense structure but with a narrowly conical shape. Although it is still suitable for the smaller garden, it is more of a focal point due to its shape and growth rate. Plant it in full sun and rich soil for the best color.

Linssen garden

Coenosium Gardens

Picea omorika 'Treblitzsch'

The many different cultivars of *Picea omorika* that developed from witches' brooms have many differences and similarities. Some of the differences are apparent only to the experts. However, *Picea omorika* 'Treblitzsch' is quite distinctive and easy to identify. As a young plant, it is compact and cushion shaped, similar to the other forms. The foliage is quite coarse with short, straight needles, a characteristic that separates it from the other dwarf forms of *Picea omorika*.

As *Picea omorika* 'Treblitzsch' ages, it becomes conical. Growing just over 1" (3 cm) per year, a twenty-year-old specimen may be about 3' (1 m) tall and almost as broad at its base. The branch structure is very dense, and multicolored foliage completely covers its exterior.

Originating as a witches' broom, *Picea omorika* 'Treblitzsch' was found in Treblitzsch Park at Beigen, Germany, about 1977. Its unique foliage and slow growth rate make it a very desirable plant for the smaller garden. It works especially well in a rock garden in full sun with the good drainage that is present in a rockery. It can also be used in borders where the dominant plants are dwarf selections from various genera.

Photo on left is at the Esteldorfer garden while the one above is at the Beran garden

Picea orientalis 'Mount Vernon'

Neil Hall and his wife, Susan, own Wells Nursery in Mount Vernon, Washington. When Dianne and I visited them in the early 1980's, Neil gave me a young plant of *Picea orientalis* 'Well's Minima'. It was a five year old propagation from a witches' broom found on a *Picea orientalis* in the city of Mount Vernon.

It traveled across the country with us to Pennsylvania and returned to the west coast when we moved to Oregon and later to our present home near Eatonville, Washington. The plant Hall gave us is still doing well and growing in one of our gardens. Somewhere along the line the name was changed to *Picea orientalis* 'Mount Vernon' since 'Well's Minima' is illegitimate.

Picea orientalis 'Mount Vernon' is a dwarf selection with a globular shape and very dense foliage, which does not scald in the full sun like some of the other ultradense spruces. It grows up to 2" (5 cm) per year in the northwestern United States but less than 1" (2 cm) per year in the northeastern United States. The tiny needles are dark green and create a different color and texture for the rock garden. My original plant, which is one of the first generation propagations, is over thirty years old and about 4' (120 cm) wide and 2' (60 cm) high.

This selection likes full sun to partial shade with well drained soil. However, if it is allowed to dry out completely during a hot summer period, it can suffer some burn. It is propagated by grafting, and although it may not be easy to find in retail garden centers, a persistent person should be able to locate it at a specialty nursery.

Coenosium Gardens both photos

Picea orientalis 'Professor Langner'

I used to think that *Picea orientalis* 'Professor Langner' was one of those miniature spruces that looked great for a few years, then burned out, and died. However, after seeing some fine specimens in Europe, I changed my mind. I have discovered that it likes a bit of afternoon shade to prevent sun scald of the foliage on exceptionally hot, summer afternoons. This is also true of most miniature selections of *Picea abies*.

'Professor Langner' is exceptionally dense and grows about 1" (2 cm) per year. It is a true miniature with a globose shape and dark, shiny green foliage with very short needles. As a young plant, the center will be slightly depressed presenting somewhat of a nest shape to the plant. As time passes, the center eventually becomes more convex. I like to think of it as a green form of *Picea orientalis* 'Tom Thumb Gold'. Plant it in an area of a rock garden where it is exposed to filtered sunlight in the afternoon.

I doubt that this plant will ever be easy to locate since only a few specialty nurseries offer it for sale, and those are mainly mail order.

Coenosium Gardens

Linnsen garden

Picea orientalis 'Tom Thumb Gold'

I remember sitting in Jean Iseli's office at Iseli Nursery in Boring, Oregon when I was visiting the West Coast in the early 1980's. Jean was very excited about the discovery of a new plant. Watching Jean in a situation like this was actually quite entertaining and part of Jean's charm. His excitement was due to the discovery of a witches' broom in a *Picea orientalis* 'Skylands' in a homeowner's front yard by one of the nursery's salesmen. He wanted to add propagations of that broom to the nursery collection. Jean was not only a plant collector but also a shrewd businessman. He knew the value of a plant that might result from this broom. At the same time, Jean was an artist who imagined the beauty such a plant would add to the garden.

A few days later Jean got the "bad news". The broom had already been spoken for by John Verkade, a nursery owner in New Jersey. Verkade had heard about the broom a year or two before Jean's salesman spotted it. Jean was actually depressed for a few days but then made plans to obtain a few small plants from Verkade Nursery. Eventually he was able to do so.

When I returned to Pennsylvania, I called John Verkade, and he offered me two young plants in trade. Verkade was one of the "old timers" in the conifer world and loved spending time with other collectors. I visited him several times over the years and worked with him when a group of us organized the American Conifer Society at Joel Spingarn's home. Verkade's specialty was *Tsuga canadensis*, and he had introduced several outstanding forms, named mostly for family members. When the two young *Picea orientalis* 'Tom Thumb Gold' plants arrived, it was like Christmas. I didn't have the heart to tell Jean that Verkade had sent me two young plants before he got his.

I planted them in full shade to prevent burning. I used them as stock plants and started producing some for sale. I gave one young plant to Larry Stanley, a close conifer friend. When I lost both of my stock plants because the shade was too dense, Larry gave me a plant from his production.

Picea orientalis 'Tom Thumb Gold' is a miniature selection with bright yellow foliage identical to that of *Picea orientalis* 'Skylands'. It grows about 1" (2 cm) per year and becomes a tight little globe or cushion. It can tolerate up to about three hours of sunlight a day, but not at the hottest part of the day. More sun will cause burning while less sun will subdue the yellow/gold coloration and make it a shade of green. Good drainage with sufficient moisture will prevent root problems while also protecting against sun scald.

Picea orientalis 'Tom Thumb Gold' was originally listed by Verkade as 'Aurea Compacta Tom Thumb', but with his permission, I renamed it 'Tom Thumb Gold'. Recently it was incorrectly changed to 'Tom Thumb' by someone who just wanted to shorten the name, causing some confusion about the correct name.

Coenosium Gardens

Linssen garden

Picea pungens 'Blue Pearl'

Picea pungens 'Fat Albert' was selected at Iseli Nusery as the best form of Colorado blue spruce to grow for the nursery trade. It developed a perfectly symmetrical shape with little or no training. The blue color was good, although not exceptional. The combination of its growth habit and Iseli salesmanship made it a popular plant at the nursery and among the nursery's customers.

Jean was always trying to grow *Picea pungens* selections from cuttings for a variety of reasons, such as a lower cost of propagation and a more compact growth habit for young plants. 'Fat Albert' showed signs of being a good choice to propagate in this manner. One year the nursery rooted almost 300,000 cuttings of this plant. Jean was ecstatic until he realized the nursery resources that were going to be tied up in this one offering. The large number of 'Fat Albert' plants did present a number of problems for many years both before and after Jean's death.

Meanwhile, one plant of 'Fat Albert' developed an exceptional witches' broom with good color and a dense growth habit. As the nursery developed the broom and prepared plants for production, they tightly controlled its distribution. It was given the name *Picea pungens* 'Blue Pearl'. The nursery eventually abandoned its production for some unknown reason.

However, plants are available from a number of sources. I was able to obtain three scions from a European friend who had visited Iseli Nursery and was given ten pieces of wood. I propagated it and was ready to offer it when the nursery named it.

Picea pungens 'Blue Pearl' is a low, dense bush with short needles and bright blue foliage. It is a miniature selection that grows just over 1" (3 cm) per year. It is equally at home in the smaller garden as a specimen or the larger garden as an accent plant.

Picea pungens 'Blaukissen' (blue cushion) is very similar with a slightly faster growth rate. It was found by Günther Eschrich, Germany in 1978 and can be used in much the same way as 'Blue Pearl'. 'Blaukissen' is pictured on the left at Linssen's garden.

Coenosium Gardens

Coenosium Gardens

Picea pungens 'Donna's Rainbow'

When Jean Iseli, his father, and brother purchased Orogreen Nursery in Boring, Oregon, it was with the idea of creating a wholesale nursery that would produce a unique product line of dwarf and rare conifers in specimen sizes. Orogreen produced large numbers of *Picea pungens* and had selected an assortment of unique plants that they grew in a special field. Periodically Jean or an employee would make a unique discovery in this field. Plants like *Picea pungens* 'Iseli Fastigiate' and *Picea pungens* 'Iseli Foxtail' were registered and introduced to the trade by Iseli Nursery.

I corresponded with Jean for a number of years before I met him. We also exchanged plants and scion wood during those formative years. He sent me a nice assortment of *Picea pungens* selections that they were working on. Some of these plants were introduced through Iseli Nursery and some were not. Among the plants he shared with me were *Picea pungens* 'Yvette' (described elsewhere in this book) and *Picea pungens* 'Donna's Rainbow', which had been found growing on the nursery by an employee named Donna.

Picea pungens 'Donna's Rainbow' is a dwarf, dense, conical plant with all of the new shoots angled sharply upward, giving it a very distinctive appearance. It grows about 3" (7 cm) per year. Its foliage is light blue with the needles slightly angled toward the tip of the branch, similar to the foxtail spruces. It can be used for some height in the medium sized rock garden or as part of the border of a smaller rock garden. As a very young plant, 'Donna's Rainbow' has a terrible shape with long and short branches shooting off at various angles. After five or six years, it starts to show promise as it tightens up and develops character.

I have yet to find a spruce to compare with the appearance of a mature *Picea pungens* 'Donna's Rainbow'. It can be used as a centerpiece in a moderately sized garden but stays small enough to blend into a rock garden or border garden planting scheme. My oldest plants are twenty years old and less than 5' (1.6 m) tall and 3' (1 m) wide. Planted in a sunny location with good drainage, 'Donna's Rainbow' will not scald and the growth will eventually be very dense.

Coenosium Gardens

Picea pungens 'Early Cones'

Many dwarf and miniature conifers do not produce cones, or if they do, the cones are rather insignificant. Since cones add greatly to the garden appeal of a conifer, finding a dwarf conifer that freely produces cones is a major event. During my 1992 visit to Australia, I found such a conifer at Ferny Creek Nursery near Victoria.

Picea pungens 'Early Cones' grows about 2" (5 cm) per year and becomes a flat topped bush twice as wide as high with cones developing at the ends of the branches, making it an 'Acrocona' variety of *Picea pungens* The cones are purplish when they first appear in the spring, drying to paper-bag brown as they mature. The gray-blue foliage consists of short, thin needles on slender branchlets. It develops slowly and needs about five years before it assumes an appealing shape. Use it in any size rock garden where a small blue cushion is wanted. Consider the cones a bonus. Found as a seedling by Peter and Joe Versteege, Ferny Creek Nursery, Victoria, it was introduced in 1992.

Interestingly enough, a similar plant was discovered a few years later in Germany. *Picea pungens* 'Hermann Naue' is almost a "dead ringer" for 'Early Cones' with a few significant differences. From a nurseryman's viewpoint, 'Hermann Naue' is a better choice since it becomes a full bush in a shorter time possibly due to its faster growth rate as a young plant.

Either selection provides a focal point in the garden that would attract much interest. Use either one in a rock garden or to complement a planting along a border or above a wall. Both plants will be difficult to find, but as time passes, their availability will become more widespread.

Linssen garden above and to the left with 'Early Cones' above and 'Hermann Naue' to the left

'Hermann Naue'
Vermeulen garden

Picea pungens 'Jean Iseli' & *Picea pungens* 'Frieda'

Edsal Wood is mentioned several times in this book. He was owner of Bonsai Village Nursery in Aurora, Oregon, and developer of Wood's Rooting Hormone. When I met him in 1984, Wood had scaled back his operation considerably. He was a pioneer in the business of growing seedlings in plug trays, and Bonsai Village Nursery was a portion of his original growing operation. He was still involved in producing conifer seedlings in fairly large numbers as well as marketing prebonsai material.

One of Wood's closest friends was Jean Iseli, the man responsible for many happenings in the world of conifers. Iseli was the first president and driving force behind the conifer powerhouse known as Iseli Nursery. He was instrumental in the formation of the American Conifer Society, and his passion for conifers ignited a similar passion in many others who came into contact with him.

When Iseli died in 1986, Wood honored him by naming several very special seedlings for him. One of these seedlings was a *Picea pungens* named 'Jean Iseli'. It is a blue-gray dwarf with a globose shape and depressed center. It grows just over 1" (3 cm) per year and does best in full sun and well drained soil. Use it in rock gardens and other locations where a small, bluish shrub will add interest to the garden.

Picea pungens 'Jean Iseli' must be carefully propagated to maintain its growth characteristics. When it is propagated from rooted cuttings, it maintains its dwarf character. When grafted, it becomes a coarse, irregularly shaped pyramidal shrub with a dull, gray-blue color.

Picea pungens 'Frieda' has a number of similarities to 'Jean Iseli' and a number of distinctive differences. Discovered by Franz Esteldorfer, Austria, and named for his wife, *Picea pungens* 'Frieda' is a dense, little globe with bright blue foliage. The needles are small and thin and densely arranged along its branchlets. It grows less than 1" (3 cm) per year as it maintains its globose shape. It must be propagated from rooted cuttings since grafting will cause it to bolt and become upright and conical with a coarse texture.

Both of these plants are very suitable for the small garden or rockery and should be planted in full sun with well drained soil. The color and shape differences allow both to be used without duplication of similar traits.

Picea pungens 'Frieda' grafted in rear and rooted to the front in the Nelis Kools garden

Picea pungens 'Frieda'
Balatka garden

Picea pungens 'Pali'

Every fifty years the Royal Horticultural Society sponsors an International Conifer Conference. In the summer of 1999 I was given the opportunity of a lifetime when I was asked to present a paper on North American conifer cultivars at their meeting in England. When a Hungarian friend, Zsolt Mesterhazy, learned I was coming to the continent, he offered to spend a week showing me the major conifer collections in the Budapest area.

One day we visited Artur Ruisz, an enthusiastic nurseryman and conifer collector. The Ruisz Nursery produces a wide variety of conifer liners. The nursery is small by western standards, but a nice sized family operation for his part of the world.

A miniature selection of *Picea pungens* named 'Pali' was, for me, the highlight of his collection. It is a very dense, globular plant with small needles and good blue color. After touring the garden, Ruisz offered us a glass of wine produced locally (I opted for juice). When we left, he made me a gift of nearly a full gallon of wine to enjoy during my Hungarian visit.

Picea pungens 'Pali' is a very interesting, dwarf selection of Colorado spruce. Not only is it slower growing than most, but it also maintains a more globose shape than most of the others, which tend to be cushion-shaped. Growing about 1" (3 cm) per year, it is reliably dwarf. Its foliage is blue, although not as bright as some.

Selected about 1975 by Mr. Pal Lengyel, *Picea pungens* 'Pali' was a seedling in Prenor Nursery, Szombathely, Hungary, and is just now appearing in gardens throughout Europe. In North America it is still quite rare and will require considerable effort to locate. It is worth the search since it has many uses in the smaller garden or rockery and is quite distinctive from other selections like 'St. Mary' or 'Blue Pearl'. Plant it in full sun in well drained soil. It tolerates dry conditions without suffering any sun scald.

Ruisz Nursery

Picea pungens 'Porcupine' and 'Yvette'

A dwarf bun of exceptionally high density, *Picea pungens* 'Porcupine' grows less than 1" (2 cm) per year. Its foliage is blue with short, stiff, sharp needles. The needles are almost longer than the annual growth, and the winter buds are so small as to be easily overlooked. It will never be easy to find because a nursery has to grow it for quite a long time before it reaches a saleable size. This investment doesn't justify the return for most nurseries since people still tend to buy plants by size, not age.

The original plant was first exhibited at The Farwest Trade Show in Portland, Oregon in the early 1980's. Jean Iseli tried to purchase it, but the owner refused to part with it. Then when Dick Bush asked for it, he just gave it to him.

Dick Bush was a close friend of Jean's. He owned Bush's Nursery and spent a lot of time sharing ideas with Jean. Bush loved to fly and owned a single engine aircraft. He would often land his airplane in an open spot at Iseli Nursery whenever he wanted to visit Jean. His plane was bright yellow and would cause a stir whenever he buzzed the main office at the nursery. Some days he flew in just to have lunch.

He seldom ever got "one up" on Jean, but this time he did. Jean was disappointed but happy that a close friend got 'Porcupine'. Dick propagated it and shared it with Jean and with me. Eventually the original plant was stepped on by a horse and lost.

The only plant that compares to it is *Picea pungens* 'Yvette', found at Iseli Nursery and named for Jean's younger daughter. It is very similar and may be used in the same way in a rock garden. Plant it wherever a tiny blue mound with dense, coarse foliage is desired. It needs good drainage, full sun, and good air circulation.

'Porcupine' at Coenosium Gardens

Picea pungens 'Yvette'
Iseli Nursery

Picea pungens 'Porcupine'
Linssen garden

Picea pungens 'R. H. Montgomery'

I am including this selection since it is often sold as a dwarf conifer. I consider it more of a compact conifer, and when used as a dwarf in the landscape, it will often outgrow its location. In fact, a friend of mine has often grown *Picea pungens* 'R. H. Montgomery' for use as Christmas trees in his own home.

During the 1930's Colonel Robert H. Montgomery owned an estate, Wild Acres, near Coscob, Connecticut. He was possibly the most active conifer collector of his era. His collection became very large, and he even tried to organize a national conifer society.

When Colonel Montgomery moved to Florida, his collection was donated to the New York Botanic Garden. In 1951 at the dedication ceremony of the Montgomery Dwarf Conifer Collection, the centerpiece was a *Picea pungens* 'R. H. Montgomery'.

Picea pungens 'R. H. Montgomery' is considered a dwarf form by many people. It is slow growing and very compact, becoming broadly conical as it develops. It grows up to 3" (8 cm) per year. The foliage is bright blue, and the needles are quite prickly.

Although *Picea pungens* 'R. H. Montgomery' is propagated by grafting, it does sporatically root from cuttings, producing a fuller, more densely branched plant. If terminal shoots are propagated, the typical conical shape quickly develops. If lateral shoots are used, then the resulting plant will be globose for many years, before assuming the typical conical growth expected from 'R. H. Montgomery'. Plants labeled as *Picea pungens* 'Glauca Globosa' are produced using lateral shoots and will not stay globose.

Picea pungens 'R. H. Montgomery' originated as a seedling before 1934 in the Eastern Nurseries, Holliston, Massachusetts, and was named *Picea pungens* 'Glauca Compacta Globosa'. I think the nursery owner wanted to be certain to include all of the growing possibilities in the name. Colonel Montgomery purchased the plant for his estate, and it was later given the name 'R. H. Montgomery' just before the New York Botanic Garden dedication.

In 1937 *Picea pungens* 'Glauca Globosa' made its appearance in a Dutch nursery. Its exact parentage has never been established, and several sources believe it originated from cuttings taken from the Montgomery plant. This probable renaming has led to considerable confusion in the nursery industry, and so plants sold as *Picea pungens* 'Glauca Globosa' invariably become pyramidal as they age.

Picea pungens 'R. H. Montgomery' is an excellent focal piece for any garden. Do not use it where it has limited growing space. With sufficient space, it will become a dense, blue pyramid that will contrast nicely with any other colors used around it.

Picea omorika 'Nana' to left and *Picea pungens* 'R. H. Montgomery' to the right at the Hillier Arboretum

Picea pungens 'St. Mary' ('St. Mary's Broom')

I first came across this plant when I was visiting Layne Ziegenfuss in Lehighton, Pennsylvania. Layne was the owner of Hillside Gardens and was responsible for introducing many new conifers during the 1960's. We spent many hours talking about conifers. Sometimes we would walk through his field and look at plants he was growing for scion wood.

In one spot he had a short row of *Picea pungens* 'St. Mary' that were about twenty years old. The plants were all less than 1' (30cm) high and three times that wide with bright blue foliage. The last year I visited Layne he told me that he was losing his oldest 'St. Mary'. The center had died, and the plant was declining. He was of the opinion that the life span of this cultivar was only about twenty years. I didn't argue with him at the time, but I knew he was wrong. That previous winter I had noticed that someone had stepped in the center of the plant and snapped or cracked many of the branches.

This bright blue cultivar was found as a witches' broom at Saint Mary's Convent in New Jersey. The original broom is in sad shape but was still alive as of 2009. It is not uncommon for specimens of this cultivar to have many buds that never push, leading to slower growing regions on the plant, producing a low cushion with an irregular outline. The winter buds are very pronounced.

Picea pungens 'St. Mary' has a variety of uses in the landscape. It can be used as a foundation planting or in a rock garden or as a blue mound to provide color in a mixed border of lower growing ornamental shrubs. It needs good drainage and prefers full sun. It will grow in partial shade but will be a bit looser in its growth habit.

Coenosium Gardens for both photos

Picea smithiana 'Ballarat'

I remember a visitor from Australia who came to our nursery in the late 1980's. This young man was Peter Nitschke. I didn't know it at the time, but he was an avid conifer explorer/collector from "down under". Nitschke was visiting us to look at our conifer collection and to discuss some of our propagation practices. He was especially interested in the propagation techniques we used for *Chamaecyparis lawsoniana*. It seemed that the Australians had the same problems we did - root disease (*Phytophthora lateralis*) and premature death. For years Nitschke had been experimenting to find a compatable understock. Since we were doing the same, we were able to compare notes. Any understock that resisted *Phytophthora lateralis* was unsuitable since the scion overgrew everything we tried.

Nitschke died a few years later, just a short time before I visited Australia on my own conifer exploration trip. While I was there, I discovered he was a very prolific plant explorer. He had introduced many excellent *Cedrus*, *Cupressus*, *Pinus*, and *Picea* cultivars through his nursery. I have several of these introductions in my own collection.

Picea smithiana 'Ballarat' was one of his discoveries. It is not suitable for cold climates but thrives in milder ones. Nitschke found it as a witches' broom on a *Picea smithiana*. 'Ballarat' develops into a diminutive, dark green mound with drooping branchlets. It is very dense and may grow up to 2" (5 cm) per year. The dark green foliage has short needles. It is a natural for the smaller rock garden with its unique drooping appearance as if it were in need of water. Plant it in the full sun in a location with good drainage for best results.

Both plants at Coenosium Gardens

Pinus banksiana 'Chippewa'

I used to visit the Arnold Arboretum in Jamaica Plain, just outside Boston, Massachusetts, whenever Dianne and I went to see her brother. I enjoyed walking through the old conifer collection and exploring the dwarf conifers near the Dana Greenhouse. I told my friend Layne Ziegenfuss about my visits, and we discussed the old conifer collections since he was very familiar with them. Ziegenfuss told me to get in touch with the former Head Propagator, a man named Al Fordham. I called Fordham and arranged a visit, and Dianne, Al, and I became close friends. I would often make trips to see him, and we would spend hours touring the arboretum and discussing the conifers.

Fordham was a pioneer in the process of growing seedlings from conifer witches' brooms. Orman Hamilton, a landscape designer and naturalist, had shown Fordham small seedlings growing beneath a witches' broom, sparking a lifelong interest. Fordham experimented for many years with witches' broom seedlings and made a number of significant findings. He theorized that 50% of the seedlings of a broom would exhibit varying degrees of dwarfness. He published his work in a series of articles for "Arnoldia", and shared it through the International Plant Propagators Society. Dr. Sidney Waxman of the University of Connecticut was a very close friend of Fordham's and shared his interest in the subject of witches' broom seedlings. He had been with Fordham when Hamilton showed them the seedlings he had found. Waxman became very interested in this topic, and grew over 100,000 witches' broom seedlings at the university. His records showed about a 50% dwarf rate among the seedlings, supporting Fordham's observations.

Fordham introduced a number of dwarf selections through the Arnold Arboretum. A.G. Johnson of Minneapolis, another close friend of Fordham's, sent him seeds from *Pinus banksiana* witches' brooms. One of the nicest and most dwarf seedlings grown from these seeds was *Pinus banksiana* 'Chippewa', which was named and introduced about 1970. Fordham believed in using Native American names for his introductions. The best of the *banksiana* witches' broom seedlings he introduced were 'Chippewa', 'Neponset', and 'Manomet'. He also introduced *Pinus strobus* 'Uncatena' and 'Merrimack' which are discussed later on.

Pinus banksiana 'Chippewa' develops into a miniature, irregular, flat-topped mound. It grows less than 1" (2 cm) per year. The foliage is light green with tiny needles mostly held parallel to its branchlets. The prominent winter buds are elongated, gray-white, and slightly resinous.

This plant makes a very hardy addition to any garden. It likes to be kept in well drained soil with full sun. It needs little attention as it is relatively pest and disease free.

Pinus banksiana 'Chippewa'
Coenosium Gardens

Pinus banksiana 'Manomet'
Coenosium Gardens

Pinus cembra 'Aurea'

Through the years I have visited Arboretum Trompenburg many times and have often been a houseguest of its owners. Dick and Riet van Hoey Smith became very close friends of ours and have always treated us like members of their family. During one of my earliest visits I came across a dense, narrow pine with a golden sheen to the foliage. Dick told me it was *Pinus cembra* 'Aurea'. The golden sheen was due to the color of the individual needles. Each one appeared to have been dipped into bright yellow paint for about one third of its length.

During winter visits I noticed the color was even more intense, but always toward the ends of the needles. *Pinus cembra* 'Aurea' is a compact, narrowly conical selection that grows about 4" (10 cm) per year. Its foliage is yellow-green during the growing season, becoming brighter in the winter. Some authorities believe the plant to be 'Aureovariegata' which originated in France. I doubt that idea is true since there are no patches of yellow foliage to give it a variegated appearance.

Pinus cembra 'Aurea' can be difficult to graft. When grafted, it grows very slowly for the first three or four years. In five or six years it assumes a more normal growth rate. Our oldest plant has attained a height of eight feet (2.6 meters) in twenty-five years.

Planting in the full sun will allow *Pinus cembra* 'Aurea' to develop its best color. It needs well drained soil; and although it does become a small, dense tree, it will stay narrow and take up little space in the garden.

Coenosium Gardens

Bloom garden

Pinus heldreichii var. *leucodermis* 'Smidtii'

During my visits to the Czech Republic there was always one plant I could count on finding in every conifer garden. *Pinus heldreichii* var. *leucodermis* 'Smidtii' is possibly the most popular conifer in that country. It is often labeled as *Pinus leucodermis*, actually a variety of *heldreichii*. For many years it went under the name `Schmidtii'. This is a Germanization of the name of its discoverer, Eugene Smidt, who found the original plant in the mountains near Sarajevo, Yugoslavia (then Bosnia) in 1926 as a 1' (3 m) tall tree estimated to be over 100 years old. It has also been grown in gardens under the incorrect name of *Pinus heldreichii* var. *leucodermis* 'Pygmy'.

Pinus heldreichii var. *leucodermis* 'Smidti' has a compact growth habit, becoming oval as it ages. It is very slow growing and densely branched. The needles are deep emerald green, maintaining this color throughout the four seasons. Some specimens will develop an upright growth habit under ideal conditions. The upright form was once thought to be a mutation so it was given other names. It is too common an occurrence for renaming and appears to be a result of a specific plant's growing conditions.

The first plant to be propagated is still growing in the Pruhonice Park near Prague. It is near the top of a very steep slope and marked off limits to visitors due to the unstable approach path. From time to time it has had to survive vandalism and must now be nearly 80 years old.

Place this plant in the full sun with well drained soil. It will maintain its rich green color without any special care and will stay small, even if it does become conical as it ages.

Coenosium Gardens

*The original propagation made about 1930
Pruhonice Arboretum*

Beran garden

Pinus mugo 'Carstens'

I first visited Jo and Maarten Bomer at their specialty nursery in Zundert, Holland, with Dick van Hoey Smith to see their collection of European beeches (Fagus sylvatica). They, along with their son, are noted for their extensive collections of beech and ginkgo trees. While there I discovered they also had a nice selection of conifers under development, many of which came from Dr. Barabits, a notable Hungarian conifer expert.

Two of their mugo pines were especially interesting. Long rows of *Pinus mugo* 'Zundert' and *Pinus mugo* 'Carstens' were growing in the nursery. These were nicely shaped plants with typical green foliage. During a visit two years later I saw the same plants in their winter colors. The 'Zundert' was bright yellow and growing like a typical *Pinus mugo* v. pumilio. The 'Carstens' was intensely gold and much dwarfer than the 'Zundert'. Both are striking additions to the winter garden.

Bomer gave me the name of this plant as 'Carstens Wintergold'. Since then some nurserymen have been calling it just 'Carstens'. So it may be found under either name. I believe that 'Carstens' is the more generally accepted name. This change was probably made to prevent confusion with a totally different plant named *Pinus mugo* 'Wintergold'.

Pinus mugo 'Carstens' is a compact, broadly globose selection that grows about 3" (7 cm) per year. Its foliage is a rich, bright gold during the winter. A number of mugo pines turn gold in the winter, but this selection is the brightest and most compact of them all.

Found by Erwin Carstens, Varel, Germany, before 1988, it does very well in the full sun and will have its best color under that condition. It needs well drained soil and in twenty years will be about 3' (1 meter) high and just slightly wider than that.

'Zundert'
Coenosium
Gardens

Pinus mugo 'Carstens' to the right and 'Jakobsen' to the left
Coenosium Gardens

Pinus mugo 'Fructata'

Karel Maly, a Czech conifer collector, lived in the village of Hvozdany. He welcomed visitors and was eager to show his conifers. Maly was always experimenting with chemicals on his firs in an attempt to induce the formation of witches' brooms. He would treat buds and cones with colchicine trying to induce chromosome doubling. He did have some congested growth on a few treated branches and several thousand fir seedlings in flats that he was just starting to observe. Unfortunately he passed away before his experimenting showed any major results.

In a planting located just behind his back porch was a dwarf, globose *Pinus mugo* with tiny cones scattered throughout the foliage. Maly told me that it was *Pinus mugo* 'Fructata', and the name meant "fruitful". The name was representative of its freely coning habit.

Pinus mugo 'Fructata' is a compact, globular selection that grows 2" (5 cm) per year. Its foliage is light green and consistently produces large numbers of small cones that stay small throughout the growing season. Originating as a witches' broom, it was discovered about 1981 by Karel Kalous in the Czech Republic.

This mugo pine stays small enough to use where space is limited and produces quantities of small cones as an added attraction. It prefers full sun and does best in well drained soil.

Coenosium Gardens

Beran garden

Maly garden

Pinus mugo 'Hvozdany'

Karel Maly was a conifer collector from the village of Hvozdany, Czech Republic, who was attempting to chemically induce witches' brooms on some of his full sized trees. He loved having visitors and always wore his American Conifer Society cap whenever I came by. As we would tour his garden, he carried a notebook that had the history of every plant in his collection.

As I am writing about Maly, I am looking at a gift he gave me during my 1996 visit. It is a decoupage butterfly, done with dyed tissuepaper on a thicker paper, and framed. Whenever I look at it, I think of Maly and how a number of my conifer collecting friends enjoyed doing art projects. It gives me another aspect of their hidden personalities. Maly passed away in 2005, but will be remembered for some of the special plants he introduced.

Maly had a number of interesting plants, and one of his smallest and best was *Pinus mugo* 'Hvozdany'. It originated from a witches' broom just a short distance from his home. It is a dense green cushion that grows less than 1" (2 cm) per year. Although it will require some searching to locate, 'Hvozdany' is well worth the effort.

Pinus mugo 'Hvozdany' is an excellent selection for a rockery or alpine setting. Use it in full sun with well drained soil and good air circulation.

Halada garden with 'Hvozdany' behind a dwarf spruce

Maly garden

Pinus mugo 'Jakobsen'

The average person's first dwarf conifer is often a mugo pine, *Pinus mugo* v. pumilio to be precise. Then when it proves to be not-so-dwarf, all mugo pines get lumped into the "plants to avoid" group. That is unfortunate since many attractive selections of *Pinus mugo* stay dwarf and grow the way the gardener expects them to grow. These are called cultivars. The variety called pumilio is a seedling selection that is kept sheared at the nursery to give it a dwarf appearance.

Pinus mugo 'Jakobsen' is a dependable selection that definitely does what is expected. I saw my first 'Jakobsen' at the Hillier Arboretum in the dwarf conifer collection. I was on my first visit to England, and Alan Mitchell was my host. I spent a week with him touring conifer collections. We had a great time, even though I was a cultivar guy and he was into species, the bigger the better. Mitchell made his reputation as an author and also as a businessman measuring the big trees of the British Isles.

While at Hillier's, I concentrated on studying the plants in the dwarf conifer gardens when I came across a *Pinus mugo* 'Jakobsen' growing beside the Hillier home. It was during the winter, and the plant was dark green with an open branch structure. Its dense foliage clustered especially thick toward the ends of the branches. It was obviously a very special plant.

Pinus mugo 'Jakobsen' is a slow-growing, broad mound with areas of exceptionally dense foliage. The branch structure is easily observed since the foliage tends to be most prominent towards the branch ends. The foliage is dark green with curved needles held tightly together. The winter buds are white, large, and blunt. They tend to form in groups of three arranged in a straight line. Thus, a typical plant displays its younger growth with a two dimensional structure rather than three dimensional. It grows about 2" (5 cm) per year and originated with Arne Vagn Jakobsen, Denmark. It is thought that 'Jakobsen' may be a hybrid of *Pinus nigra* and *Pinus mugo* due to its dark green foliage and pure white winter buds.

Pinus mugo 'Jakobsen' prefers the full sun and well drained soil. It will eventually attain a width of about 6' (2 m) and a height of 3' (1m). Use it where you would like to have an irregular mound of dark green with a branch structure that is almost alpine in appearance. Its lumpy outline is definitely not for the formal garden.

Coenosium Gardens

Pinus mugo 'Little Delight'

Pinus mugo 'Mops' has a tendency to produce witches' brooms. Several such brooms have been named, propagated, and introduced into the nursery trade. One of these brooms appeared on a *Pinus mugo* 'Mops' at a nursery we owned in Canby, Oregon in 1989. Employees were taking cuttings for summer propagation when they spotted the broom. I had them trim around it, and I grafted it that winter. The resulting plant turned out to be very special.

Pinus mugo 'Little Delight' was my first popular introduction. I was able to follow it with *Picea glauca* 'Beehive', *Picea mariana* 'Blue Teardrop', and *Picea abies* 'Gold Drift', all very special plants. Being able to introduce new plants is a dream of every conifer collector. I have worked with conifers a long time and have been able to make these and several other introductions. I am not a witches' broom fanatic and have made my discoveries either by accident or by deliberate cross pollination of plants in my collection.

Pinus mugo 'Little Delight' is a most appropriate name for this plant. It develops into a miniature globe. The growth rate is about 1" (2 cm) per year with a dense branching habit and small, thin needles. It will be a 2' (60 cm) globe after about twenty-five years. The foliage is green, and it prefers full sun along with well drained soil. Use it in a rock garden or any other area highlighting miniature to dwarf plants.

Two little mugo pines from the Czech Republic can be used in the same settings as 'Little Delight'. They are also very slow and develop into dense little globes. One of them, *Pinus mugo* 'Nerost', is a dwarf, broadly globular selection that at ten years may be 14" (35cm) wide by 8" (20cm) high. It has green foliage and short needles. 'Nerost' originated as a seedling grown in 1992 by Daniel Pesek at Kutna Hora, Czech Republic. Pesek wanted to give a descriptive name to the plant as well as show a little humor. He used the name 'Nerost', which means "does not grow".

The other, *Pinus mugo* 'Sleizsky Dom', is both very choice and very difficult to find. At twelve years it will be a dwarf, low, rounded globe 10" (25cm) wide by 10" (25cm) high. Its foliage is dark green, and the plant is exceptionally dense. 'Sleizsky Dom' originated as a witches' broom and was found by Bohomil Kroc in the High Tatra Mountains of the Czech Republic about 1976. This name means "mountain hut".

'Little Delight'
Stanley & Sons Nursery

Original broom at Mitsch Nursery

Pinus mugo 'Nerost' in the Linssen garden

Pinus mugo 'Nerost' planted in a stone trough in the Beran garden

Pinus mugo 'Sleizsky Dom' planted in a rock garden among several alpines in the Halada garden

Pinus mugo 'Sherwood Compact'

Oregon's nurseries have always produced *Pinus mugo* v. pumilio seedlings in large quantities. When a seedling variation occurs, it will occasionally be identified as such and held back from sales. Many of these variations are missed because the plants are kept sheared and aren't allowed to show any special growth characteristics.

Andy Sherwood, a nurseryman near Portland, Oregon, was good at spotting unusual plants and introduced a number of plants to the Oregon nursery industry. Perhaps the best known is the golden Noble fir, *Abies procera* 'Sherwoodii'. *Pinus mugo* 'Sherwood Compact' was another one of his introductions. It was found as a seedling and introduced about 1960, but in spite of its special attributes, it is not as well known.

Pinus mugo 'Sherwood Compact' will propagate from rooted cuttings, but with mixed results. As with many rooted conifers, the plants with be smaller and denser. Grafting of *Pinus mugo* 'Sherwood Compact' will produce faster growing plants when young, but as the root-to-shoot balance re-establishes itself, the growth rate will slow.

Also called 'Teeny' in some lists, *Pinus mugo* 'Sherwood Compact' becomes a dense, symmetrical globe. It grows about 2" (5 cm) per year. Its foliage is dark green with needles arranged radially around each branch. Use it in any garden where a dark green globe with a twenty year diameter of 2'-3' (1 meter) is desired.

Pinus mugo 'Michelle' is a new introduction that was found as a witches' broom on 'Sherwood Compact'. It is a dense, tiny bun with twisted needles. The winter buds are prominently interspersed throughout the bright green foliage. It is becoming readily available since its introduction by Iseli Nursery, Boring, Oregon. 'Michelle' is perfect for troughs, small container plantings, and rock gardens.

'Sherwood Compact'
Iseli Nursery

'Sherwood Compact' at Coenosium Gardens

'Michelle' in Linssen garden

Pinus nigra 'Oriesok'

Pinus nigra, the Austrian pine, is a very attractive species but only has a few named cultivars that stay reliably small. The species also has a few problems in North America. In the Midwestern United States it is subject to a particularly nasty disease causing widespread death among the Austrian and Scots pines throughout the region. The vector that carries the disease is a wood boring beetle. This beetle only bores into trees while dwarf, shrubby forms like 'Oriesok' are ignored.

Pinus nigra 'Oriesok' is a dense, little plant that grows about 2" (5cm) per year. As it ages, it takes on more of a conical shape, becoming a dense, little pyramid with light green foliage. It originated as a witches' broom that was discovered in 1981 by Jaroslav Kazbal at Rodopy, Bulgaria. The small, tight broom on the large tree led Kazbal to use 'Oriesok' as its name, since the term means "little nut".

Use *Pinus nigra* 'Oriesok' in garden locations where some upright structure is desired. It does best in full sun and needs good drainage.

There are two alternatives to 'Oriesok' that can serve the same purpose in the landscape. The first, *Pinus nigra* 'Black Prince', is not as narrowly conical. Growing up to 3" (8 cm) per year, it is slow-growing, dense, and pyramidal. Its foliage is green with short, straight needles. Originating at Chantry Nursery, Honiton, Devon, England, it became part of the National Dwarf Conifer Collection at Windsor Great Park, where I first saw it.

The other alternative was found as a witches' broom in Marktheidenfeld Germany, in 1965. Growing as much as 3" (8 cm) per year, *Pinus nigra* 'Helga' is a dwarf, upright selection with bright white winter buds and long green needles. Many nurseries describe 'Helga' as a dwarf globe. That description is correct for a young plant, but it does develop an upright habit as it matures.

Pinus nigra 'Helga'
Beran garden

Pinus nigra 'Oriesok'
Coenosium Gardens

Pinus nigra 'Black Prince'
South Seattle Community College Coenosium Rock Garden

The *Pinus nigra* of Henri Bregeon, Renens, Switzerland

I first saw *Pinus nigra* 'Pipouniou' on a trip through several European countries with my good friend Larry Stanley. It was one of several miniature and dwarf *Pinus nigra* cultivars that caught our attention. A number of these miniatures and dwarfs arose through the efforts of Henri Bregeon of Renens, Switzerland. In the 1970's he crossed *Pinus densiflora* 'Umbraculifera' with *Pinus nigra* 'Nana' and selected several special plants from the many seedlings that resulted from the cross. *Pinus nigra* 'Pipouniou' was one. Among the others were *Pinus nigra* 'Pichounet', 'Pierrick Bregeon' ('Brepo'), 'Gaelle Bregeon' ('Bambino'), and 'Marie Bregeon'.

As a young plant, 'Pipouniou' is a dense, shaggy, little mop head. It grows just over 1" (2 cm) per year for the first five to seven years. Then it will take on more of the typical *Pinus nigra* appearance with longer needles held radially around each branch. The growth rate is closer to 2" (5 cm) per year with each shoot having light green needles projecting straight outward around each shoot. The large, light tan buds make a nice contrast to the foliage.

Pinus nigra 'Pichounet' is a sister seedling of 'Pipouniou' and shares some of its characteristics with a few differences. The biggest difference is the appearance of short branches with clusters of short needles around the terminal buds on older plants. This characteristic creates a different texture for the garden since most of the plant will have normal branches and foliage.

I enjoy having both of these plants in the garden, but I had problems with the spelling of their names until I corresponded with Clement Antoine in Belgium who corrected the names for me. It is often difficult to spell plant names in an unfamiliar language. Even so, it is important not to change the name simply to make it more familiar.

Place these plants in full sun with well drained soil. They are excellent choices for the small garden, such as a rockery or a container garden. Be careful not to let them be overgrown by fast growing annuals or perennials.

'Pipouniou'
Coenosium Gardens

'Pichounet'
Beran garden

> **The *Pinus nigra* of Henri Bregeon, Renens, Switzerland**
> (cont.)

The other plants grown by Bregeon are not as dwarf but are easier to find and purchase. *Pinus nigra* 'Marie Bregeon' has a plant patent recorded for it. It has a nice round shape without pruning and light green, spiraling needles. The needles are surrounded by light gray stipules in the winter. It grows almost 3" (8 cm) per year. The buds are cylindrical and range in color from light brown in summer to gray in the winter with pointy tips. It is densely branched and appears to be very disease resistant, probably due to its hybrid ancestry with *Pinus densiflora*.

Pinus nigra 'Pierrick Bregeon' ('Brepo') and 'Gaelle Bregeon' ('Bambino') are similar to 'Marie Bregeon' in a number of ways but do have some distinct differences. *Pinus nigra* 'Marie Bregeon' is rounder than Pinus 'Gaelle Bregeon' and 'Pierrick Bregeon'. The mature needles of *Pinus nigra* 'Marie Bregeon' are more spirally formed and are lighter green than the foilage of both *Pinus nigra* 'Gaelle Bregeon' and 'Pierrick Bregeon'. The needles also last three to four years on 'Marie Bregeon' compared to two to three years on *Pinus nigra* 'Gaelle Bregeon' and 'Pierrick Bregeon'. The stipules around the needles of *Pinus nigra* 'Gaelle Bregeon' and 'Pierrick Bregeon' are brown, and their growth rates are faster. Both 'Gaelle Bregeon' and 'Pierrick Bregeon' have a light resin production from their buds while 'Marie Bregeon' has none.

Pinus nigra 'Pierrick Bregeon' ('Brepo') grows 4" (10 cm) per year, developing a rounded shape that tends to be broader than high. It is densely branched with long, green needles. It is being produced in large numbers in North America by at least one large wholesale nursery. It does best in full sun with well drained soils.

Pinus nigra 'Gaelle Bregeon' ('Bambino') grows up to 4" (10 cm) per year developing a rounded shape that tends to be broader than high. It is densely branched with short, green needles. It does best in full sun with well drained soils.

The names 'Brepo' and 'Bambino' are not the correct cultivar names for these plants. They are names used to inhance their commercial potential. The name 'Brepo' was legally registered as a synonym name while 'Bambino' was not. When a cultivar is given a name through publication or registration, it cannot (should not?) be changed. However, trademarking or registering another name for commercial reasons is allowed. Unfortunately, that means one plant may have any number of names. I have tried to use original cultivar names as much as possible in this book. I only mention other names to illustrate some of the confusion in the world of conifer nomenclature.

'Gaelle Bregeon' ('Bambino')
Stanley & Sons Nursery

'Pierrick Bregeon' ('Brepo')
Helms garden

Pinus parviflora 'Burke's Bonsai'

I visited Joe Reis several times a year during my conifer exploration trips to Long Island, New York. Several times Reis told me that I just had to visit a guy named Joe Burke, who lived about a half hour away in Merrick. When I was finally able to find the time to visit Burke, I discovered a free spirit who became a good friend until he suddenly passed away.

Burke was a U.S. Marine fighter pilot during WWII who adopted a whole new outlook on life when he landed his plane upside down on Saipan. He loved life and loved his plants, especially bonsai plants. Burke shared some very special plants with me that make striking landscape plants for the larger garden. He grew *Pinus parviflora* seedlings as understock and selected several with special attributes.

Burke was an expert grafter and taught me a number of his grafting techniques, such as grafting into the root crown for bonsai production. Burke also showed me how to sharpen a grafting knife and encouraged me to use high quality knives.

Burke planned to move to the Northwest because he figured if a nuclear war broke out, he could avoid the fallout. He also had a great appreciation for precision machinery and collected old sewing machines. He loved the challenge of repairing them.

One of the *Pinus parviflora* seedlings Burke grew had very short needles with an open growth habit. Burke was propagating it for use as bonsai. I saw a greater potential for it for landscape use in the smaller or larger garden. The thin, short needles and open branching habit meant it could provide height in the smaller garden without shading any understory plants. Burke had never named the plant. When I suggested calling it *Pinus parviflora* 'Burke's Bonsai', he agreed and sold me several small plants.

Pinus parviflora 'Burke's Bonsai' is a selection that is an irregularly growing, open branched, small tree. It has a proclivity for producing adventitious buds on up to three year old branches creating areas of dense foliage. It grows up to 8" (20 cm) per year in the landscape. Its foliage is dark green with short, straight, thin needles. Cones are common throughout the plant. They are smaller than the species; and although they open normally, I am uncertain if they produce viable seed.

Although it is an excellent selection for a garden with an oriental theme, it can be used in any size or type of garden in full sun with well drained soil.

Coenosium Gardens

Pinus parviflora 'Glauca Nana'

Although it is not a miniature, *Pinus parviflora* 'Glauca Nana' is a plant that does not take up much space in the garden. It is a narrow, open, irregularly growing little tree. It grows about 6" (15 cm) per year. The foliage is bluish green with short, straight needles. The branches grow more upright than horizontal, contributing to its narrow growth habit.

Although the majority of dwarfs tend to be more bush-like or cushion-like, there are a number of dwarf conifers that are upright. The fact that *Pinus parviflora* 'Glauca Nana' is a narrow, small, upright tree makes it an exceptionally valuable selection for the smaller garden.

Pinus parviflora 'Glauca Nana' also produces viable seed. When Al Fordham was the head propagator at the Arnold Arboretum, he was visiting friends who had a *Pinus parviflora* 'Glauca Nana' in their landscape. It had a single cone on it. Fordham picked the cone and took it back to the arboretum where he removed several seeds. One of these seeds produced a dwarf seedling that now bears Fordham's name: *Pinus parviflora* 'Al Fordham'.

Pinus parviflora 'Glauca Nana' has also produced a number of miniature seedlings at an Oregon wholesale nursery. Working with a large crop of *Pinus parviflora* 'Glauca Nana' seedlings, the nursery was able to make a number of interesting selections. None has ever been considered for introduction to the nursery trade although a collector may obtain one from time to time.

Consider *Pinus parviflora* 'Glauca Nana' for a sunny spot in the garden and watch for cones. Seedlings from dwarf conifers can produce some interesting plants. At the same time, it will be a nice addition to an informal garden where it can add a rustic atmosphere with its irregularly upright growth habit.

Pinus parviflora 'Al Fordham' at Coenosium Gardens

Coenosium Gardens

Pinus parviflora 'Hagoromo'

I always enjoyed visiting with Gunter Horstmann at his home in Germany. His conifer collection had a great variety of interesting plants. He specialized in dwarf and miniature forms, many of which he discovered as witches' brooms in various countries throughout the world. He also gathered plants from other European collectors.

During one of my visits, I noticed a dwarf *Pinus parviflora* with small cones. It was the first time I had seen a dwarf of this species. Gunter told me it was a seedling called *Pinus parviflora* 'Hagoromo' that he had gotten from another collector, Tage Lundell of Helsingborg, Sweden.

Pinus parviflora 'Hagoromo' is a dwarf selection that develops into a dense, globose bush, becoming more conical as it ages. Many of the branches will have small cones develop at their terminal ends. The foliage is bluish with short, strongly twisted needles. The growth rate is about 2" (5 cm) per year.

This plant has long been one of my favorites, but it does appear to have a problem. I have always propagated it by grafting onto *Pinus strobus*. This understock works well for *Pinus parviflora*, but sudden death is not uncommon for established plants. Analysis seldom reveals any disease or insect problems, and the compatibility appears to be satisfactory. However, *Pinus parviflora* 'Hagoromo' seems to have a survivability rate of only about twenty years. I have had universal loss of old plants, grafted at ground level and grafted onto 3' (1 m) high standards. Other collectors I have talked to have the same problem. This may be a plant that has a definite life span. If it does, twenty years is a good length of time since most landscapes need renovation after that long anyway.

Use it in full sun with good drainage. It makes a definite statement in any landscape while using just a small area of the garden.

Coenosium Rock Garden at South Seattle Community College

Pinus parviflora 'Kobe'

Pinus parviflora 'Kobe' has been part of my conifer collection for twenty years. I hadn't paid much attention to it until a friend, Don Howse, asked if I still had it in my collection. His had died, and he was looking for another. He mentioned that it was a nice, little upright form of *Pinus parviflora* so he wanted to replace it.

I found my older plant in an area of my garden where it was overshadowed by some larger conifers. It was so attractive that I took three plants from inventory, gave one to Don, and planted the other two in other garden areas.

Pinus parviflora 'Kobe' is a selection that is slow-growing and conical with straight, thick yellow-green leaves. The branching is dense enough to create a full appearing tree. It will be 6' (2 m) high and about 3' (1 m) wide in twenty years. *Pinus parviflora* 'Kobe' was introduced by Edinburgh Royal Botanic Garden, Scotland, who imported it from the Kobe Arboretum, Tokyo, Japan.

Plant *Pinus parviflora* 'Kobe' in sunny locations with good drainage where you want a more formal, small, conical *Pinus parviflora*.

Coenosium Gardens both photos

Pinus parviflora 'Pygmy Yatsubusa'

At the Arnold Arboretum in the early 1970's I discovered a dwarf *Pinus parviflora* with an Arnold Arboretum designation number on it. Upon investigation I learned it was *Pinus parviflora* 'Adcock's Dwarf', a plant that originated in the early 1960's at the Hillier Nursery in England. The head gardener, Graham Adcock, had grown several *Pinus parviflora* seedlings; and when a well known collector expressed interest in one of them, he kept it under observation and eventually named it.

Pinus parviflora 'Adcock's Dwarf' is a dwarf form, very slow growing and compact. Its needles are short and thin, gray-green, clustered and crowded at the branch tips. It can grow as a dwarf, densely branched shrub or more upright as a narrowly conical little tree-like bush. Don Smith of Watnong Nursery in New Jersey showed me both forms.

A few years later, on a visit to purchase plants from Joel Spingarn on Long Island, I discovered another pine that could easily be mistaken for 'Adcock's Dwarf'. It was *Pinus parviflora* 'Pygmy Yatsubusa'. I don't know the origin of this plant, but its growth habit is intermediate between the two extremes of 'Adcock's Dwarf' (see next page). A dwarf selection, 'Pygmy Yatsubusa' becomes a dense, miniature tree with no effort on the part of its owner. It is usually single-trunked with a central leader and dense branching. It grows up to 3" (8 cm) per year. It has light green foliage with short, twisted needles and pronounced winter buds. My oldest plant is 5' (3.6 m) high by 3' (1 m) wide after twenty years.

I have come to prefer 'Pygmy Yatsubusa' as a good garden plant for the Northwest since it will seldom defoliate in the spring, a problem that is very common with 'Adcock's Dwarf'. I have never seen this problem in other parts of North America. I believe it is due to our wet, cold winters and springs. It is a fungal attack that only affects the older foliage of 'Adcock's Dwarf'.

Use *Pinus parviflora* 'Pygmy Yatsubusa' or 'Adcock's Dwarf' wherever a dense, little pine fits into the landscape. Both prefer full sun with well drained soil and good air circulation. A period of extreme cold in the winter may cause the foliage to suffer browning but should not kill either plant.

'Pygmy Yatsubusa'
Coenosium Gardens

Pinus parviflora 'Adcock's Dwarf'

This specimen, growing at Mitsch Nursery, Oregon, shows the upright habit that more commonly occurs with this cultivar.

This specimen, growing at Arboretum Trompenburg in Holland, shows the lower, spreading habit that can occur.

Pinus parviflora 'Tanima-no-yuki'

Early in my collecting career I heard of Michael Kristick who lived in the area where I went to college. I paid him a visit and discovered that Kristick had known Fred Bergman of Raraflora Nursery. Bergman had an exceptional conifer collection that essentially disappeared upon his death. It was auctioned off and scattered around North America. Kristick was able to propagate many of the plants from Bergman's collection and offered a number of them for sale.

Kristick had one plant that especially fascinated me. Bergman had imported it from Japan, and Kristick was able to make it part of his collection. *Pinus parviflora* 'Tanima-no-yuki' has a variegation that is unique in the world of conifers. The new growth in the spring consists of pink candles surrounded by white foliage. Kristick only had a stock plant, but he agreed to propagate a graft for me. When I received it the following year, it was a small thing attached to a rather large seedling. I grew it for three years before I completely removed the seedling.

Pinus parviflora 'Tanima-no-yuki' is a selection that develops into a dense, upright, bush. It can grow up to 3" (7 cm) per year once it becomes established. However, that sort of growth is erratic and does not occur every year. Most of the growth is much less, and the plant will be very densely branched although it may attain a height of 3' (1 m) in ten to fifteen years. It is possibly the most colorful of this species with the white variegation being profusely painted throughout its green foliage. The spring growth first appears pink and the first needles are white, making a colorful display.

When *Pinus parviflora* 'Tanima-no-yuki' is propagated by grafting, the understock must be left on for up to three years since it lacks sufficient green foliage and strength to maintain the borrowed root system of the understock. It needs afternoon shade to develop the purest white without burning. It also needs well drained soil.

Due to the slow growth rate and difficulty of establishing a newly propagated plant, *Pinus parviflora* 'Tanima-no-yuki' will never be widely available and must be obtained from a specialty nursery.

Iseli Nursery

Pinus parviflora Witches' Brooms

Witches' brooms in conifers have proven a valuable source for dwarf and miniature conifers, both from their seed and their asexual propagation. It is very interesting that one species of conifer, *Pinus parviflora*, is very prolific at producing seedling mutations but has only produced a few witches' brooms. One of these rarities is *Pinus parviflora* 'Tsai's Cushion'; another is *Pinus parviflora* 'Regenhold'.

Pinus parviflora 'Tsai's Cushion' was given to me by Tsai Cheng, who is best known for her work with Japanese maples. She gave me a plant that was grafted on a standard and was growing less than 1" (2 cm) per year with short, thin needles that had slight twists near their ends. Propagations have proven tricky to establish, and I obtain the best results when I gradually remove the understock over a period of three to five years. I named the plant in her honor.

This cultivar is a congested ball of twisted, light green foliage. The branches are short and thin with many tiny winter buds. The needles need to be periodically cleaned out to allow air circulation through the plant. For best results, the graft union should be at least several inches above ground. It is a good choice for the small rock garden or for a trough.

I once grafted twenty scions onto the top branches of an eight foot (1.7 m) tall *Pinus strobus*. The energy of the understock pushed each scion to thicken and grow almost 4" (10 cm) long. Each one then produced dozens of winter buds and thick clusters of accelerated shoots. This growth rate has been going on for over five years and is just starting to slightly slow down. The propagations from this plant will revert to what is normal for *Pinus parviflora* 'Tsai's Cushion'.

I first saw *Pinus parviflora* 'Regenhold' in the collection of a Dutch friend, Ronald Vermeulen. Interestingly enough, when we discussed his plant, I learned that it was from a witches' broom discovered by Ronald Regenhold from Cincinnati, Ohio.

I have always been slightly amazed at the number of plants I have observed in European gardens, which were new to me, and yet, had originated in the United States. 'Regenhold' is one such plant. Growing up to 2" (5 cm) per year, *Pinus parviflora* 'Regenhold' becomes a dense globe with exceptionally blue, twisted foliage. It prefers full sun with well drained soil, and works very well in a rockery or even in a mixed garden of smaller growing plants.

'Tsai's Cushion' at Coenosium Gardens

'Regenhold' in the Vermeulen garden

Pinus strobiformis 'Loma Linda'

Jerry Morris is a name known by conifer enthusiasts as the most prolific collector of witches' brooms in North America. Morris has found thousands of brooms throughout the mountains of the western United States. Mainly working with brooms of *Abies concolor, Abies lasiocarpa, Picea pungens* and *englemannii, Pinus aristata, Pinus flexilis, Pinus edulis, Pinus strobiformis, Pinus ponderosa* and *Pseudotsuga menziesii,* Morris has distributed scions and seeds throughout the country.

Pinus strobiformis 'Loma Linda' is one of Morris' finds. It does not grow in a manner that we expect from a plant of witches' broom origin. A witches' broom is generally a dense mass of branches or foliage in a tree. The mass tends toward a somewhat spherical shape as it ages. Occasionally one will develop an upright growth habit. Propagations from brooms tend to mimic the shape and growth rate of the broom. However, there are exceptions, and some plants do grow differently from the parent broom.

It is thought by some taxonomists that *Pinus strobiformis* 'Loma Linda' is actually *Pinus reflexa*. Whichever one it may be, 'Loma Linda' is a very choice selection of hardy, five-needle pine. It is a densely branched, upright, narrow conical little tree. It grows 4" to 5" (10 cm to 12 cm) per year with clusters of buds at the ends of the branches. The long needled foliage is soft textured with an attractive blue-green color. In twenty years a plant might be 5' (1.6 m) tall by half as wide.

Pinus strobiformis 'Loma Linda' is an excellent choice for any size garden. It can be used wherever a dense, mid-sized cone with an irregular outline and a soft texture can make a statement. It thrives in full sun and well drained soil.

Helms garden

Pinus strobus 'Horsford'

During the 1960's a very special plant was found in New England. In the wilds of Vermont William Horsford discovered a *Pinus strobus* growing that had formed a tight, little cushion. He moved the plant onto his own property where he could watch it. He was a friend of Greg Williams and shared scion wood with him and Layne Ziegenfuss of Hillside Gardens Nursery. The plant was quickly available in the nursery trade from a few conifer specialists.

Pinus strobus 'Horsford' soon became the standard for evaluating other dwarf forms of pine. It is a miniature selection that becomes a cushion-shaped, dense little bun. Growing about 2" (5 cm) per year, it has light green foliage with relatively long, thin needles and short annual growth, giving it the appearance of a shaggy little cushion. I suspect this seedling's origin was as a witches' broom seedling. I don't know if Horsford ever searched for one in the area where the seedling was found.

I obtained a *Pinus strobus* 'Horsford' at my first opportunity, and it has always been a part of my collection. As it grew to a larger size, I used to cut the plant very hard every winter for scion wood. I deliberately cut holes into the plant for air circulation. The following spring the plant filled in the holes showing no sign of the severe pruning. When I discovered that larger plants were consistently dying throughout the Northeast, I recommended that everyone do severe winter pruning. As with most miniature *Pinus strobus*, it has to be cleaned of dead needles each winter or sudden death often occurs in the spring, a problem common to all dwarf bun forms of *Pinus strobus*.

The original plant no longer exists. Horsford planted it near his home in a field that also served as a horse pasture, and it was stepped on and smashed sometime in the 1980's. *Pinus strobus* 'Horsford' is an excellent little plant for any sized landscape. It is extremely hardy, prefers sunny locations with good air circulation, and needs well drained soil.

Pinus strobus 'Greg' and *Pinus strobus* 'Uncatena' are very similar to 'Horsford' and can be used in the same way in the landscape. Both of these selections were selected as witches' broom seedlings. Greg Williams selected the one, which he sent to someone on Long Island, New York, who affixed Greg's name to it when it was distributed to collectors. Al Fordham selected and named the other plant as part of his studies of witches' broom seedlings.

Pinus strobus 'Greg' has shorter needles than 'Horsford', and short needles tend to form around the terminal buds for the winter. 'Uncatena' has shorter needles and a slightly faster growth rate than 'Horsford'. Both will enhance any landscape.

'Horsford' grafted on a standard
Helms garden

'Greg'
Arboretum Trompenburg

Pinus strobus 'Merrimack'

Al Fordham worked with and studied witches' broom seedlings at the Arnold Arboretum. He named a few very special selections during his tenure as Head Propagator there. *Pinus banksiana* and *Pinus strobus* were two areas of focus.

Whenever Fordham named one of his introductions, he used Native American names. He believed that the first Americans were close to nature and had a way of naming things that reflected their best natural aspects. Merrimack was an Indian word for 'winding river', and Fordham used it for an exceptional witches' broom seedling that he grew and introduced about 1970.

Pinus strobus 'Merrimack' is a dwarf, dense globular plant that grows broader than high. The foliage is so dense that the plant needs to be "cleaned" out each winter so that the dead needles don't block air circulation and encourage fungal problems.

Pinus strobus 'Merrimack' grows at a relatively slow rate of about 2" (5 cm) per year. Its foliage is green, becoming yellowish-green during the winter. This seasonal color change is one of the identifying characteristics that add to the appeal of this cultivar.

Use this plant in the landscape where a soft, green cushion that changes color with the seasons is desired. It does best in the full sun with good air circulation and well drained soil.

A similar plant, also named by Fordham, was *Pinus strobus* 'Uncatena'. It can be used in much the same way as 'Merrimack'. It has the same shape as 'Merrimack' but grows more slowly without the winter color change.

'Merrimack'
Arnold Arboretum

'Merrimack' on the left and 'Uncatena' on the right at Iseli Nursery

Pinus strobus 'Mini Twists'

Greg Williams and Layne Ziegenfuss were very good friends. Both were very active during the 1960's and 1970's finding and introducing new conifers to the nursery trade. Many introductions were made through Layne's Hillside Gardens Nursery. Ziegenfuss has been gone for a number of years while Williams remains active at his Vermont home locating unusual conifers in the wild as well as developing his own new forms from seed.

Early on, Williams discovered that *Pinus strobus* 'Horsham', a dwarf selection from a witches' broom, produced viable seed with a high percentage of dwarf seedlings. He grew a number of these seedlings and even named a few that he felt were worthy of introduction.

Pinus strobus 'Torulosa' is an open-branched tree with serpentine branches and twisted needles. It is attractive but becomes quite large. Williams had a *Pinus strobus* 'Horsham' planted near a 'Torulosa' and worked with its seedlings for a number of years. A high percentage of these seedlings were dwarf and exhibited characteristics inherited from the 'Torulosa'. Williams shared three of these seedlings with other collectors and nurserymen. I was one of the collectors.

When I wanted to introduce two of the seedlings through Coenosium Gardens, I contacted Williams and received his permission to name them. I named the slowest growing seedling 'Mini Twists'. The faster growing seedling, called 'Tiny Kurls' by Dianne, was introduced first. The fastest growing seedling of the three never became popular and wasn't given a name.

Pinus strobus 'Mini Twists' develops into a dense little bush with an extensive branching habit. The strongly twisted foliage is green with silver-blue stripes and forms a thick covering that hides the branch structure. It will grow about 2" to 3" (5 cm to 7 cm) per year in the Northwest but less than that in other parts of the United States. Older plants will be slightly rounded and almost as wide as high.

Give *Pinus strobus* 'Mini Twists' plenty of light and well drained soil for it to perform at its best. Use it in a rock garden of as part of a shrub border where it can compete with smaller growing perennials.

Coenosium Gardens

Pinus strobus 'Sarah Rachel'

Dr. Sidney Waxman of the University of Connecticut, sent me scion wood from a plant he had named for his daughter along with some other scions I had requested. I grafted the wood and grew the plant for several years in a container. It never impressed me very much, but in 1998 I did put two of them into our garden, and then proceeded to forget about them, inadvertently ignoring them for the next six or seven years.

In 2007 I was working on a project when a dwarf *Pinus strobus* caught my eye. It was shaped much like a dwarf Alberta spruce, dense and narrowly conical. I searched for the label, which read *Pinus strobus* 'Sarah Rachel'. I then realized that I had gotten a real prize from Waxman.

I am not aware of any *Pinus strobus* selection that will be just 6' (3 m) tall and half that width and be completely clothed in foliage when almost twenty years old. *Pinus strobus* 'Sarah Rachel' is a perfect choice for many locations in the landscape where a dense, conical lttle tree can make a statement.

Pinus strobus 'Sarah Rachel' grows just over 4" (10 cm) per year and has a dense branch structure. The foliage completely hides its interior. As a young plant, it is rather nondescript and easily overlooked. However, as it ages, its uniqueness and desireability become apparent. The light green color and the soft textured, long needles create a very pleasing effect.

Plant *Pinus strobus* 'Sarah Rachel' in full sun with well drained soil. It will provide a vertical aspect to any garden, although the smallest garden might need to use it as a background plant.

Coenosium Gardens

Pinus strobus 'Sea Urchin'

During the late 1970's Al Fordham suggested I visit Dr. Sidney Waxman at the University of Connecticut. When I visited Waxman and had a tour of his facility, I was amazed. There were thousands of witches' broom seedlings growing in long, straight rows. He had been working with them long enough that he was starting to make some selections.

His first introductions were selections of *Pinus strobus*. He showed me all of the original plants (*Pinus strobus* 'UConn', 'Green Shadow', 'Blue Shag', and 'Sea Urchin'), and I arranged for him to send me scion wood from all of them. Over the years *Pinus strobus* 'Blue Shag' has become a popular replacement for *Pinus strobus* 'Nana' due to its similar growth rate and improved color. Two of the others, 'UConn' and 'Green Shadow', have seen limited popularity, possibly due to their faster growth rates.

Pinus strobus 'Sea Urchin' is the most dwarf of all of Waxman's introductions. He found it was more difficult to propagate than the others, but its diminutive size and excellent color have made it a popular choice for smaller gardens. Its slow growth rate means that the "quick buck" nurseries will not produce it, but enough of the better nurseries offer it to make it relatively easy to locate.

Pinus strobus 'Sea Urchin' is a very dwarf shrub that develops into a very dense, low, bluish mound. It grows about 2" (5 cm) per year, and its foliage is bluish-green with short needles. Each year before the new growth appears, the old needles need to be cleaned out from the interior of the plant. All of the dwarf *Pinus strobus* tend to trap their old, fallen needles inside which can lead to disease problems.

Use *Pinus strobus* 'Sea Urchin' wherever a bluish cushion is desired in the garden. It is a wonderful choice for a rock garden or a miniature conifer garden or a foundation planting. Do not mix it with larger growing perennials since they will tend to smother it.

Esteldorfer garden

Koemans garden showing 'Sea Urchin' near the base of *Juniperus communis* 'Compressa'

Pinus sylvestris 'Bennett Compact'

William Bennett lived in Virginia and was a master at discovering unusual plants growing along the highway as he traveled. He was an instructor at VMI and had a keen eye for unusual conifers. It was he who discovered the original *Pinus virginiana* 'Wate's Golden' and *Pinus strobus* 'Bennett O.D.' ('Bergman's Variegated') among many others.

Layne Ziegenfuss and Greg Williams came to know Bennett very well and had access to all of his discoveries. I am not certain how they met him, but it may have been through Fred Bergman who had a then famous collection of conifers near Philadelphia, Pennsylvania.

When I became close friends with Layne Ziegenfuss, we used to spend time on the hill behind his house where he had hundreds of rare conifers growing in old fruit juice cans. These were from the days before plastic containers came into widespread use. We would study and discuss many interesting plants, and eventually Ziegenfuss sold me all of his duplicates, and I had the core of what would soon become an outstanding conifer collection.

One of the plants Ziegenfuss parted with was an interesting dwarf Scots pine called *Pinus sylvestris* 'Bennett Compact'. It was in one of the gallon fruit juice cans, stunted, off color, but obviously very special. I planted it in one of my gardens, and in a few years I had a very special little conifer.

Discovered by William Bennett in the 1960's, *Pinus sylvestris* 'Bennett Compact' is a miniature selection that becomes a dense, irregular little mound. It will grow about 2" (5 cm) per year with an occasional shoot of up to 4" (10 cm) most commonly in colder climates. Its foliage consists of relatively long, stiff, thick, sharp needles with a basic color of blue to gray with undertones of green. The winter buds are large and white with evidence of ample resin production. The needles are often longer than the annual growth on most of the branches. I have several plants that are over twenty years old, and each is about 3' (1 m) tall by half that wide.

The special color, squatly conical shape, coarse needles, and dense branching structure make this a perfect plant for any informal garden, especially rock or alpine gardens. Plant it in the full sun with good drainage, and it will live a long life with little care.

Coenosium Gardens

Pinus sylvestris 'Jeremy' and "friends"

One of the larger conifer collections in England belongs to Gordon Haddow. He not only has been very active collecting conifers, but he also was involved with Humphrey Welch and the publication of Welch's conifer data in the form of a checklist. Haddow planned to collect every known conifer cultivar and put together the largest collection in the world. When we visited with him in the early 1980's, he was well on his way at a place he called Kenwith Castle, a combination nursery and planned bed & breakfast.

When we toured his gardens, I noticed quite a few striking plants. Three dwarf selections of *Pinus sylvestris* were especially nice: *Pinus sylvestris* 'Jeremy', *Pinus sylvestris* 'Pixie', and *Pinus sylvestris* 'Little Ann'. All three were dwarf, compact, and densely branched, with obvious differences.

Pinus sylvestris 'Jeremy' is a compact, broadly globular selection. It grows up to 3" (7 cm) per year. Its foliage is dark green with short, straight needles and prominent, bright brown, pointed winter buds. 'Jeremy' originated from a witches' broom found at Wellingborough, Northants, England, by B. Reynolds in 1973.

Pinus sylvestris 'Pixie' is a dense, globular selection that grows about 2" (5 cm) per year. It tends to become somewhat conical as it ages but retains its dense branching habit. Its foliage is green with short leaves. It was found by Don Hatch, Chantry Nursery, Honiton, Devon, England.

Pinus sylvestris 'Little Ann' is also dwarf and quite dense. It is a little globe with a flattened top and stays that way as it ages. The terminal buds are surrounded by white resin apparently exuded as the buds harden off for the winter. The resin coats the bases of the nearby needles and provides an identifying characteristic for this cultivar. It will grow about 2" (5 cm) per year with dark green foliage and short needles. 'Little Ann' originated from a group of witches' broom seedlings grown by J. D. Hoste, Manchester, England, about 1970.

All three of these selections are very reliable in their growth. They do not speed up as they age and maintain their dense structure. All three are perfect selections for the smaller garden and do best in full sun with well drained soil. 'Little Ann' is globose with a flattened top and resinous branch tips while 'Jeremy' is a more symmetrical globe, and 'Pixie' goes from globose to squatly conical.

'Jeremy' at Coenosium Gardens

'Pixie' in the Coenosium Rock Garden
at South Seattle Community College

Pinus sylvestris 'Globosa Viridis' and 'Moseri'

I remember the first time I sold a plant out of my conifer collection. The year was 1982, and we were living in Lehighton, Pennsylvania. We had visitors from Staunton, Virginia. Two of them were the Hangers, Jim and his father, Brownie. Brownie saw my oldest *Pinus sylvestris* 'Globosa Viridis', which also goes by the name 'Viridis Compacta', and just fell in love with the unique foliage character. I dug it for him and wrapped the ball in burlap. Then we had to squeeze it into the trunk of their car for the trip back to Virginia. If it wouldn't have fit, I think Jim might have had to take the bus home!

Several conifer cultivars have multiple names. That leads to some confusion and is unfortunate. 'Globosa Viridis' has even been called *Pinus nigra* 'Pygmaea', adding further to the problem. When someone realized that it was not *Pinus nigra* 'Pygmaea', a debate over its true species ensued. The name *Pinus sylvestris* 'Globosa Viridis' is still used in some lists. Then, to add to the confusion, the name 'Viridis Compacta' is used almost as often as 'Globosa Viridis'.

Pinus sylvestris 'Globosa Viridis' is a dwarf form, at first globose then becoming more conical as it develops. These were the important factors used to derive its scientific name. Unfortunately this plant also is known by two other names. These other names are incorrect but are still found on labels in gardens. One name, *Pinus sylvestris* 'Viridis Compacta' was given to it since it is green and compact. However, the actual plant given this name was supposedly a plant with a more treelike shape. Somehow that name was applied to this cultivar, perhaps by Hornibrook, who might have been basing his plant description upon a branch of 'Globosa Viridis'. The third name was given to it when it was first imported into America fifty years ago. Whoever shipped the plant from Europe had it mislabeled as *Pinus nigra* 'Pygmaea' based upon a 1923 description by Hornibrook.

Pinus sylvestris 'Globosa Viridis' will grow about 2" to 3" (5 cm to 8 cm) per year, attaining a height of about 3' (1 m) in approximately fifteen years. It is densely branched with many smaller twigs growing from the main branches in various directions. The foliage is dark green with a pronounced twist to the needles. New, short needles are formed during the summer. These needles surround the winter buds. The two different sets of needles create a very unusual feature unique to 'Globosa Viridis' and another cultivar named 'Moseri'.

During the summer months *Pinus sylvestris* 'Moseri' is easily mistaken for 'Globosa Viridis' since they are so similar. Their foliages are identical, and the only barely discernable difference is the shape. *Pinus sylvestris* 'Moseri' grows wider and lower than 'Globosa Viridis'. During the winter, however, the difference is striking. *Pinus sylvestris* 'Moseri' becomes gold, adding brightness to the winter garden. They both like full sun and well drained soils.

Pinus sylvestris 'Moseri'
Coenosium Gardens

Pinus sylvestris from Sweden

Brita and Carl-Erik Johannsen live in Sweden and have been very involved with conifer research and introductions. Brita is a well known author in her native country and is very particular when choosing new plants for introduction. Actively searching for witches' brooms among their native *Pinus sylvestris*, the couple has discovered over 150 and have propagated less than fifty of them. Three of their smaller discoveries have very special attributes that make them wonderful additions to the dwarf conifer garden.

Pinus sylvestris 'Calle' and 'Cerik' are two of the three. Both were found as witches' brooms by Carl-Erik on Halleberg, a small mountain in Sweden. 'Calle', the slower of the two, grows about 1" (2.5 cm) per year, becoming a dense globe with light green foliage. 'Cerik' will grow up to 2" (5 cm) per year, also becoming a dense globe with darker green foliage than 'Calle'. Both cultivars will thrive in full sun when planted in well drained soil. Use them in a rock garden or as part of a trough garden. They do not like to be crowded by perennials or annuals whose lush foliage produces excessive shade.

Pinus sylvestris 'Hexguld' is the third of the dwarf selections. It was found near Vanersborg, Sweden, by Carl-Erik as a golden witches' broom. The broom was twenty-five years old and attached to the tree by a stem that was only ½" (17 mm) in diameter. It is a unique plant for a number of reasons. No other dwarf pines have golden foliage. The foliage remains gold throughout the year, intensifying during the winter. It grows just over 1" (3 cm) per year, becoming a dense globe and adding a splash of gold to the smaller garden. 'Hexguld' is also interesting because it is a male broom. Anyone interested in growing dwarf conifers from seed would find 'Hexguld' a very valuable source of very special pollen.

Pinus sylvestris 'Hexguld' is not as densely branched as 'Calle' and 'Cerik' so it will not be as full. It also means that scion wood is more difficult to obtain so the plant will always be in short supply and require some searching to obtain.

These three additions to the conifer palette from Sweden are exceptionally choice and will be valuable assets to any garden.

'Cerik' at Coenosium Gardens

'Calle' at Vermeulen garden

Pinus thunbergiana 'Ogi'

Pinus thunbergiana 'Ogi' is an exceptionally dwarf selection of Japanese black pine. It is presently the only *thunbergiana* cultivar I would recommend for the smaller garden. I remember the first time I saw it. I was visiting with Eddie Rezek at his home on Long Island when he showed me his newest acquisition, *Pinus thunbergiana* 'Ogi'. At the time it was a small mound about 1' (30 cm) across. It had a coarse outline due to its slow growth rate and long, dark green needles. I admired it and commented on its slow growth rate for a Japanese black pine.

When Rezek told me to take a closer look, I couldn't believe what I saw. There were fasciations in the foliage. It was as if several of the small branches were held together by a membrane. The curved edge of each fasciation had several buds and needles. I tried every ploy to get a scion or graft from Eddie but was never able to obtain it.

A few years later I met a bonsai enthusiast, Steve Pilacik. At the time we had a mutual friend who gave me Pilacik's name and address. Pilacik was, and still is, an authority on using *Pinus thunbergiana* for bonsai. When I visited him at his home near Philadelphia, he showed me an old specimen of *Pinus thunbergiana* 'Ogi' that had been trained for bonsai. He even had a few young grafts for sale. When I returned home, I added two plants of 'Ogi' to my collection.

Pinus thunbergiana 'Ogi' is a very dense, dwarf selection that can grow up to 3" (8 cm) per year, although most years it grows less than 1" (2 cm). Its foliage is dark green with relatively long needles. Its stems have a tendency to develop as fasciations (cockscombs) with scattered normal shoots allowing the plant to increase its size each year.

Pinus thunbergiana 'Ogi' benefits from full sun with good air circulation and well drained soil. It will occasionally develop a small area of dead foliage that needs to be cleaned out. Overall, it is a fine addition to the small garden and a conversation piece due to its fasciations.

Many taxonomists prefer to use *thunbergii* for this species name. However, I have always accepted the argument put forth by Edward Cope of the L. H. Bailey Hortorium at Cornell University favoring the name of *thunbergiana*. I accepted his argument for a number of reasons that I will not go into at this time. The United States National Arboetum also accepted his reasoning. Right or wrong, both names refer to the Japanese black pine.

Coenosium Gardens

Coenosium Gardens

Pinus uncinata 'Paradekissen'

Gunter Horstmann, Schneverdingen, Germany, was a good friend who had an amazing collection of dwarf and miniature conifers as well as a number of very special larger growing conifers. When Dianne and I first visited Horstmann, we had to join him and his wife, Elisabeth, in a round of schnapps before we could tour the garden. Dick van Hoey Smith, who was driving us to various European gardens, enjoyed the scnapps. Dianne and I both got a bit teary-eyed, but not due to emotions.

One of the plants that impressed me while touring Horstmann's collection was *Pinus uncinata* 'Paradekissen'. It was about 18" (50 cm) tall and at least twice as wide. Horstmann had collected it from an alpine valley and estimated it to be over 400 years old.

In my collection 'Paradekissen' has shown a very interesting growth pattern. When it is first propagated by grafting, its diameter will be about 9" (25 cm) in three years. Then the rate slows considerably, and after a few more years it is growing less than 1" (3 cm) per year.

Pinus uncinata 'Paradekissen' is a dense, miniature, low cushion, growing about .5" (1 cm) per year as an older plant. My original plant is now about thirty years old and is 18" (50 cm)) wide and 9" (25 cm) high. It is flat-topped with small, green needles and prominent, small, pointed brown winter buds.

Pinus uncinata 'Paradekissen' is an excellent selection for the rockery or an alpine setting. Use it in full sun with well drained soil.

'Paradekissen' foliage

Linssen garden

The San Sebastian Connection

The modern Czech Republic is a center of new dwarf conifer discoveries. A number of avid explorers are constantly searching the forest for witches' brooms. Most of their discoveries are in the *Picea abies, Pinus mugo,* and *Pinus uncinata* species with additional discoveries in several other species. The brooms they find often create excellent forms for the smaller garden. The plants are usually given names that are related to either the discoverer or the location of the discovery. The San Sebastian series, however, is an exception to these naming methods.

In the San Sebastian region of northern Bohemia, Milan Halada discovered a marshy area with many specimens of *Pinus x pseudopumilio*, a hybrid of *Pinus mugo* and *Pinus uncinata*. He collected wood from a witches' broom known as San Sebastian #13, which he named 'Adam'. Since then, he and a friend, Jan Beran, have returned many times and collected a variety of witches' brooms in this area. These are known throughout Europe and America as the San Sebastian Series. Three of the slowest growing selections become dense, little cushions:

San Sebastian #2	'Babay' 1982	50cm wide by 40cm high in 15 years
San Sebastian #16	'Eva' 1989	12cm wide by 10cm high in 8 years
San Sebastian #24	'Xenie' 1987	25cm wide by 15cm high in 10 years

The last time I visited the Czech Republic, one of the conifer collectors was at San Sebastian #600+ in his collection. Another was trying to have an area planted with an example of every San Sebastian plant and had already filled over an acre of ground. The San Sebastian region has become a center of activity for many of the Czech 'broomers'. The total number of collected brooms is in excess of 1,300, all of which have been propagated and are being grown in several locations.

Many of these San Sebastian conifers have similar growth habits. Most will eventually disappear as a few selected ones will become popular and widely grown. Until then, confusion will not be uncommon. The three mentioned above are as good as any of the pines with a cushion-like growth habit and a very dense foliage and branch structure.

There are additional selections of *Pinus uncinata* from the Czech Republic that fill many niches for the small garden. Ranging from cushions to globes to small pyramids, they should be used in the full sun with well drained soil and are ideal for smaller gardens such as rockeries and troughs.

Among the *Pinus uncinata* that are not part of the San Sebastian series, *Pinus uncinata* 'Jezek' is one of the best. It is of witches' broom origin, but separate from the San Sebastian series. It is a dense, low, globose selection with green foliage, growing just over 1" (3 cm) per year. It was discovered by Mr. Kastelnicek in the Czech Republic near Krusne Hory in 1986. Its name means" hedgehog".

'Babay' at Coenosium Gardens

'Jesek' at Coenosium Gardens

Pseudotsuga menziesii 'Little Jon'

Pseudotsuga menziesii 'Little Jon' was registered with the Arnold Arboretum in 1969 after it was discovered by Albert Ziegler near Wrightsville, Pennsylvania, in 1967. Ziegler also discovered *Pseudotsuga menziesii* 'Graceful Grace' which was growing at the Masonic Home in Elizabethtown, Pennsylvania. He planted 'Little Jon' close to it, and the two of them created an exceptional landscape feature along one of the Home's access roads. Unfortunately, they were both removed for a road expansion about 2002.

'Little Jon' is a dwarf selection that is globose when young, becoming somewhat conical as it ages. Growing about 2" (5 cm) per year, its dense branching and light green foliage with brown, pointed buds, create an upright feature for the smaller garden.

Not performing as nicely in Northwest gardens, 'Little Jon' is nonetheless a good selection for most parts of North America and Europe. It prefers full sun and will thin out in shadier locations. It is evidently a cultivar from the more mountainous strains of *Pseudotsuga menziesii* since it performs better on the East Coast than the West Coast. I have observed that the inland strains of *Pseudotsuga menziesii* dislike the cool, wet winters and springs of the Northwest. Likewise, the coastal strains *Pseudotsuga menziesii* do not survive the colder climates of the middle and eastern United States.

Original plant at the Masonic Home

Taxus baccata 'Fastigiate Micro'

The English yew is very common throughout Europe, and its wood was used for the famous English longbow. Many ancient specimens are found in old church yards, with the oldest specimens in Europe being at least 2,000 years old. The wood, needles, and seeds are poisonous while the red pulp surrounding the seeds is actually sweet and popular with birds. Some English bow makers may even have died from constant contact with the poisonous wood. The oldest wood artifact ever found was yew wood and may be almost half a million years old.

There are hundreds of cultivars of *Taxus baccata* to be found throughout the world. They serve many functions in the landscape due to their tolerance of a wide range of conditions. They will grow in poor soils with good drainage and tolerate full sun to almost full shade. Of course, a nice full plant requires sunlight.

Among the dwarf forms of *Taxus baccata*, 'Fastigiate Micro' ('Fastigiata Micro' syn. ill.)is an exceptional choice of a narrowly conical plant for the smaller garden. It was selected from a block of seedlings in 1982 by Erwin Carstens, Varel, Germany. When established, it will grow about 2" (5 cm) per year into a small, narrow pillar with dark green foliage and small, thin needles. It is perfect in a small rockery or even a trough garden.

Taxus baccata 'Fastigiate Micro' is often propagated by grafting to speed up the growth for the first few years. Larger numbers can be more cheaply propagated from cuttings but require more time to reach a marketable size.

Taxus baccata 'Goldener Zwerg' is a similar plant that is more broadly columnar than 'Fastigiate Micro'. It is a slow growing selection with short, gold margined needles. Gold margined needles are not all that uncommon among the yews, but most of them will grow to a fairly large size and may not be suitable for a smaller garden. 'Goldener Zwerg' is a recent European introduction that has found its way to America. Suitable for smaller gardens, it grows about 2" (5 cm) per year becoming a dense little column.

The gold is not as striking as some forms of *Taxus baccata* and is most apparent upon closer inspection. 'Goldener Zwerg' can be used in rockeries and other smaller landscape settings where a touch of gold can provide contrast.

'Fastigiate Micro' above and 'Goldener Zwerg' to the left are both at Coenosium Gardens

Taxus baccata 'Fowle'

When I started collecting conifers, I used to be a regular visitor at Watnong Nursery, a very special place owned by Don and Hazel Smith. Located in Northern New Jersey and specializing in rare and dwarf conifers, it specialized in *Chamaecyparis obtusa* and *Tsuga canadensis* cultivars that Don rooted himself. The nursery also offered a nice assortment of pines and spruce purchased from Layne Ziegenfuss as grafted liners.

Don was a retired school administrator and Hazel was his secretary, who later became his wife. Both had been retired for a number of years before I met them. I was an oddity to them. I was in my twenties and enthusiastic about collecting and eventually selling rare and unusual conifers. I was always made welcome and often shared lunch with them.

Watnong Nursery specialized in container grown stock and also had a small area for growing larger plants in the ground. During one of my spring visits, I noticed Don's "dead" plant pile had a live yew sitting on the top that was mainly bare branches. I asked Don about it, and he told me that the deer had feasted that winter and destroyed it. It was a *Taxus baccata* 'Fowle' that he had been growing for about ten years. I asked him if I could try to salvage it; he was happy to part with it. Most of the roots had some dirt on them, and the little bit of remaining foliage was still green. I took it home and planted it. In two years it looked just great.

A semi-dwarf selection that becomes vase-shaped with a flat top, 'Fowle' produces multiple stems from a short trunk. It grows about 3" (8 cm) per year. Its foliage is adpressed and dark green. Originating as a seedling about 1950, the original plant is at the Arnold Arboretum, Jamaica Plain, Massachusetts, where it was registered in 1965.

Taxus baccata 'Adpressa Aurea' is very much like 'Fowle' with a slightly faster growth rate and yellow margined foliage. The bark on the new growth is yellow as well. It makes a nice color contrast with 'Fowle'. Originating in England about 1885, it should be fairly common in landscapes, but it is not. Locating plants to buy is difficult but well worth the time and effort.

One of the problems that contributes to the rarity of both 'Fowle' and "Adpressa Aurea' is the need to graft them. Neither one will develop roots on its own with any consistency. Both can be used in settings ranging from partial shade to full sun. The gold will not burn on 'Adpressa Aurea', and the full sun simply intensifies the variegation. Both need good drainage and may be used in rock gardens or, as they develop some size, in a border garden among small annuals.

'Fowle' at Coenosium Gardens

'Adpressa Aurea' at Esteldorfer garden

Taxus baccata 'Green Diamond'

Taxus baccata is a very useful species for a wide variety of landscape uses. Its dark green foliage and tolerance for a wide range of soils and light conditions make it suitable for some difficult locations.

Taxus baccata 'Green Diamond' is a dwarf, dense, globose selection with a flattened top that grows about 1" (3 cm) per year. Its foliage is dark green with small, pointed needles. Originating as a seedling by J. Philipsen, Helenaveen, Holland, about 1970, it has a number of excellent uses in the smaller landscape.

Many of the *Taxus* selections that are planted in home landscapes have to be regularly sheared to maintain a useful shape and size. A dense, globose *Taxus* that can be used in a rock garden, as part of a foundation planting, or as part of a landscape feature made up of a variety of dwarf and miniature forms is a valuable garden asset. 'Green Diamond' is such a plant.

It may be difficult to find, but *Taxus baccata* 'Green Diamond' is well worth the search. As time passes, it should become easier to locate as more nurseries will be producing it to meet the demand.

Coenosium Gardens

Thuja occidentalis 'Spiralis Mini'

I once spent a week traveling through part of Hungary with several friends. One of the places we visited was the nursery and home of the late Dr. Elemer Barabits. Dr. Barabits managed to operate a conifer nursery during the time Hungary was dominated by a Communistic government that valued agricultural crops and discouraged the production of ornamental plants. Dr. Barabits was very adept at developing new cultivars and is responsible for the introduction of a wide range of *Chamaecyparis lawsoniana* cultivars as well as a number of *Abies, Picea pungens, Pinus nigra*, and *Thuja occidentalis* selections.

After touring his garden, we went to his nursery and looked at a number of his discoveries. Most were planted in the ground and had become quite large. Then we looked at a number of potted plants. One he was especially proud of was a *Thuja occidentalis* witches' broom from a cultivar named 'Spiralis'. The plant was about 3' (1 m) tall and almost twenty years old. Barabits had named it *Thuja occidentalis* 'Spiralis Mini' ('Mini Spiral' syn.) to reflect its size and also its parentage, which was obvious since it was, in essence, a miniaturized 'Spiralis'.

Thuja occidentalis 'Spiralis Mini' is a narrowly conical, compact dwarf selection that grows up to 2" (5 cm) per year. Its foliage is dark green with a very fine texture and held in twisted, flattened sprays. It is a wonderful selection for the smaller garden where a small, narrow pillar is desired. The flattened, twisted sprays are a bonus.

If a more conical plant is desired, *Thuja occidentalis* 'Miky' looks more typical but grows less than 4" (10 cm) per year. 'Miky' was discovered before 1990 by Miklos Barabits as a dwarf mutation on 'Holmstrup' and was introduced that same year by Bohmer Nursery, Zundert, Holland. It is denser than 'Mini Spiral' and does not have any twist to its foliage. It is also considerable broader and grows faster than 'Mini Spiral' but will be reliably dwarf in the landscape for many years.

Use both of these cultivars in sunny locations with well drained soils. They will tolerate heavier soils than most conifers. Some searching will be required to locate either of these two with 'Miky' probably being easier to find.

'Spiralis Mini' at
Coenosium Gardens

'Miky' in the
Coenosium Rock
Garden at South Seattle
Community College

Tsuga canadensis 'Bacon Cristate'

A number of dwarf to miniature, upright Canadian hemlocks have twisted branch tips. They are very similar in appearance but differ in growth rates. Possibly the most dwarf member of this group would be *Tsuga canadensis* 'Bacon Cristate', one of a number of extremely dwarf cristate hemlocks found in the wild in northern New Jersey about 1925 by Ralph Bacon. Don Smith, Watnong Nursery, Morris Plains, New Jersey, a friend of Bacon's, worked with the original seedlings selecting and registering the best one from the group.

Smith, a hemlock enthusiast, offered a wide range of *Tsuga canadensis* cultivars for sale, many of which he rooted in a "Nearing Frame" as described in an early issue of the "North American Rock Garden Society Bulletin". In fact, when he died, Smith had a project underway that involved rooting three sets of 100 different hemlock cultivars with the idea of donating them to arboreta to grow on as reference collections. He felt that the best comparisons could be made if all of the plants in a set were the same age.

Smith was impressed with *Tsuga canadensis* 'Bacon Cristate'. He propagated a number of them both for sale and for distribution to arboreta. He compared it to the more widely known *Tsuga canadensis* 'Jervis' but as a better selection since it is much more cristate and more dwarf since it only grows about 1"(2 cm) per year. Its foliage is dark green with congested, twisted tips on the new shoots.

Tsuga canadensis 'Bacon Cristate' can be planted in partial to mostly shady locations in smaller or mid-sized gardens.

Valley Garden

Tsuga canadensis 'Betty Rose'

Tsuga canadensis 'Betty Rose' is the smallest of the white-tipped hemlocks. It is a dwarf, irregularly conical selection which grows about 1" (3 cm) per year. The spring growth, which is the primary growth, and the late summer growth, which is the secondary growth, are both white. This is an usual feature since white tipped hemlocks show their color on the secondary growth only. The leaves are irregularly spaced along the branches and point forward more than usual. The original plant was discovered near Vanceboro, Maine, by Francis J. Heckman of Ambler, Pennsylvania, and named for his wife.

I met Heckman when I lived in Pennsylvania. Layne Ziegenfuss had told me about Frank Mitsch who lived near Philadelphia and had a "dig your own plant" nursery operation. I used to visit there several times a year to dig *Thuja occidentalis* cultivars for my little retail nursery. Mitsch mentioned a friend of his who had this very special little hemlock. I got directions and telephoned Heckman. He welcomed me and showed me the original *Tsuga canadensis* 'Betty Rose'. I realized immediately that it was one-of-a-kind.

Tsuga canadensis is very diverse and has produced an inordinate number of mutations and named cultivars. In fact, it was the first widely collected species in eastern North America for garden use, and many of the early collectors specialized in this species. *Tsuga canadensis* 'Betty Rose' is the only one thus far to exhibit two flushes of white foliage and stay so small. I featured it as the cover plant of the first issue of the American Conifer Society's Bulletin. I was the first editor and wrote many of the earlier articles.

The original plant in the Frank Heckman garden (above) and a plant at Coenosium Gardens to the left showing the accelerated growth rate that is very common with conifers grown in Oregon and Washington.

Tsuga canadensis 'Cole'

Tsuga canadensis `Cole' ('Cole's Prostrate') is a selection of Canadian hemlock that has been around for a long time, but is still difficult to locate with any regularity. It was originally collected by H. R. Cole in 1929 at the foot of Mount Madison in New Hampshire. Cole was an avid hemlock collector who was actively looking for unique selections of *Tsuga canadensis*. He worked with a number of people who collected hemlock seedlings in the wild, several of whom were very good at finding mutations. The number of *Tsuga canadensis* cultivars increased at a very rapid pace through the 1930's into the 1950's.

The year 1932 was an important one in North American horticulture. The date July 1, 1932 saw the inaugural issue of "The Hemlock Arboretum at 'Far Country' Bulletin". This free quarterly publication was produced by Charles F. Jenkins, an avid *Tsuga* collector and the owner of Far Country" in Germantown, Pennsylvania. Seventy-four issues of this publication spanning almost twenty years were mailed free to anyone requesting them.

Jenkins was a hemlock fanatic. He tried to collect every hemlock cultivar in existence and wrote about the hemlocks in his collection and the events taking place at "Far Country". The discovery of new hemlocks and visitations by notable nurserymen and other hemlock collectors are documented from the early 1930's through his death in 1951. Many hemlock cultivars became well known through his efforts. *Tsuga canadensis* 'Cole' was one of these.

'Cole' grows flat along the ground and, over a period of time, will display bare, contorted branches at its center. Its foliage is dark green and will rot if the branch tips are allowed to turn downward, touching the ground. If staked, this cultivar will show an increased growth rate and avoid rotted branch tips. The full sun can scald the exposed branches at the center of the plant as it ages so it needs at least afternoon shade. It will be about 3' (1 m) wide in twenty years, but only 6" (15 cm) high.

Tsuga heterophylla 'Thorson's Weeping' is a selection of western hemlock that creates a prostrate mat with a habit similar to *Tsuga canadensis* 'Cole'. It grows about 4" (10 cm) per year over the ground and can be grown to cascade over rocks and walls. If it is staked to a certain height, it will grow at an accelerated rate and then cascade down from the top of the stake. Most prostrate conifers will accelerate their growth rates when they are staked. 'Thorson's Weeping' was introduced about 1990 by Richard Bush, Canby, Oregon.

Both *Tsuga canadensis* `Cole' and *heterophylla* 'Thorson's Weeping' are perfect for the smaller garden, especially over rocks or down a slope or over a wall. They will also add to a water feature with a "flowing" growth habit.

'Cole' at the Helms garden

'Thorson's Weeping' at Coenosium Gardens

Tsuga canadensis 'Everitt Golden'

I was able to purchase a small *Tsuga canadensis* 'Everitt Golden' from Don Smith's Watnong Nursery in New Jersey soon after I started collecting conifers. I was very pleased with myself since golden conifers were not all that common, and this one was very choice. About one year later I met Joe Reis, a conifer collector from Merrick, Long Island, New York. His garden was very small and full of special conifers that he had collected over a forty year time span. Just off to one side of his home was a 10' (3 m) tall *Tsuga canadensis* 'Everitt Golden' with no sign of burn and bright yellow foliage. Joe told me it was at least thirty years old.

A number of Northeast nurseries had been producing this plant for over thirty years, and it was still hard to locate. It could be found under a variety of names such as 'Aurea Compacta', 'Aurea', and 'Everitt's Aurea Compacta'. The most common propagation method was grafting, which resulted in compatability problems and persistent losses throughout the crop over a number of years as the grafts failed. Hemlocks have always proven to have low survival rates when grafted, so most nurseries now propagate them strictly from cuttings.

A dwarf, dense, narrow pyramid in the sun, *Tsuga canadensis* 'Everitt Golden' is dark green and fairly open when grown in heavy shade, while in partial shade its foliage is golden yellow in spring, becoming a bronze gold color in the fall. It has a tendency to burn when grown in the full sun, especially on hot summer afternoons. Found in 1918 on an exposed slope near Eaton, New Hampshire, by Samuel A. Everitt, its photo with a detailed description was published in a magazine in 1925. It was quickly added to the "must have" list of Charles Jenkins and became an early addition to his Hemlock Arboretum at Far Country.

Growing about 3" (8 cm) per year, *Tsuga canadensis* 'Everitt Golden' becomes a dense, columnar shrub. In ten years, it will be about 3' (1 m) tall, with bright yellow foliage. It needs some sun for the best color and can become a focal point in the smaller to mid-sized garden.

Heartland Collection

Tsuga canadensis 'Horsford Contorted'

Found by William C. Horsford in a pasture in Vermont, *Tsuga canadensis* 'Horsford Contorted' originated with a tree which was 50-60 feet (15-20 m) high (since cut down). The tree had slightly twisted branches, contorted branchlets, and brown, pubescent tips. Seedlings with similar characteristics were growing throughout the area. Horsford showed this tree and its seedlings to Layne Ziegenfuss and Greg Williams. One of the more compact seedlings, just over 7' (2 m) tall, with twisted foliage was selected, and cuttings were taken for propagation.

'Horsford Contorted' is a compact plant that has its branchlets twisted into tight coils and knots with very pubescent shoot tips much like those of *Tsuga canadensis* 'Cinnamomea'. As the branches mature, many of them do partially untwist. It grows up to 3" (8 cm) per year with dark green foliage and narrow needles. It will grow almost as broad as high and, like all of the *Tsuga canadensis*, prefers a partially shaded location with good drainage.

Since *Tsuga canadensis* 'Horsford Contorted' is not a miniature, it can be used in a garden among other plants for an interesting mixed planting. It does very well under the same conditions as azaleas and rhododendrons and can share their garden space but should not be crowded.

As a side note, Fred Bergman of Raraflora Nursery was able to obtain cutting wood from William Horsford and listed this plant in his 1970 catalog. At some point he changed the name to 'Pigtail', and *Tsuga canadensis* 'Horsford Contorted' will sometimes be incorrectly sold under that name.

Coenosium Gardens

Tsuga canadensis 'Jacqueline Verkade'

Before I started propagating my own conifers and had "trading material", I was constantly looking for sources where I could purchase rare and unusual conifers. I discovered a nursery called Palette Gardens about thirty miles (48 km) south of our Pennsylvania home. I visited there several times to see what was available. Quite a few of their plants were new grafts that I recognized as having come from Layne Ziegenfuss.

Ziegenfuss was the supplier of unusual grafted conifers to a number of retail nurseries throughout the Northeast. I wasn't surprised to discover that Palette Gardens was one of his customers. Ziegenfuss sold his grafted conifers to them for $1.50 each, and they would resell each plant, often in the same styrofoam cup, for $20.00 and up.

On one of my visits I discovered a hemlock with unusual foliage named *Tsuga canadensis* 'Jacqueline Verkade'. It was a dense little shrub in a large container. The foliage was unusual and immediately caught my eye. The leaves were small and scattered along the branchlets creating the appearance of a juvenile foliaged *Platycladus orientalis* (oriental arborvitae). I purchased this specimen and added it to our Pennsylvania garden.

Growing about 2" (5 cm) per year with a broadly conical shape 'Jacqueline Verkade' is very densely branched. The dark green foliage maintains its color throughout the year. It can be grown in the sun and will not burn in summer or winter. It was discovered in the seed beds at Verkade's Nursery, Wayne, New Jersey, as a three-year-old seedling in 1961.

Tsuga canadensis 'Jacqueline Verkade' is an excellent choice for the smaller garden, especially for the rock garden. It will stay reliably small and not outgrow its location while adding a healthy, dark green color to the garden as a tidy little shrub with pleasing foliage.

Reis garden

Tsuga canadensis 'Jervis'

Port Jervis is in the state of New Jersey, and G. G. Nearing of Metuchen, New Jersey, discovered a very special Canadian hemlock near that city. Nearing is noted for his work with rhododendrons, but he also found the dwarf forms of *Tsuga canadensis* to be fascinating. In 1943 he came across one that was 7' (2 m) tall that he calculated to be at least 150 years old. It was in bad condition, but he managed to take two small layers (rooted branches) and eventually shared one with Edward Thuem of Harrington Park, New Jersey, which was eventually lost.

John Swartley advised Nearing to sell it as 'Hussi', which was done with grafts made by Thuem from his original plant. Later both Swartley and Nearing agreed that was a mistake since 'Jervis' has a much denser branch structure and slower growth rate. Thuem then used a corrected name, *Tsuga canadensis* 'Nearing', for the remaining few grafted plants that he sold. That mistake and subsequent nomenclatural tinkering, has led to some confusion as to the correct name for Nearing's discovery.

Having lost the original propagation material, and realizing just how good the plant was, Nearing tried to locate the original plant once again. After several trips, he found it again in the mid 1950's only to discover that it had been even more damaged by fire and shade. He was able to take branch ends on additional trips and propagated several hundred cuttings over a period of several years. A 5" (12 cm) branch tip would typically provide almost 50 cuttings. He would not graft it since that propagation method accelerated its growth.

In 1956, the name *Tsuga canadensis* 'Jervis' was applied to young plants sold by Fred Bergman through his nursery in Feasterville, Pennsylvania. Other young plants were being sold by Thuem under the name of *Tsuga canadensis* 'Nearing'. Of the two names, *Tsuga canadensis* 'Jervis' has become widely known and is presently the accepted name for this plant.

Tsuga canadensis 'Jervis' is a dwarf form with a compressed growth habit. It is exceptionally slow growing with a dense branch structure that produces many tiny, twiggy branchlets. The branches are irregular arranged, giving a mature plant an uneven, conical outline. It is upright and may be 3' (1 m) tall by half that width in twenty years. The foliage is made up of dark green needles that are very small, crowded, and unevenly arranged along the branches with increased congestion at the tips hiding the small and inconspicuous buds.

It will tolerate partial shade to full sun in most climates and can be used as a minispecimen in the smaller gardens or as an upright feature in a rockery.

Sturm garden

Tsuga canadensis 'Minuta' and its "Friends"

Tsuga canadensis 'Minuta' was first described in 1935 by Henry Teuscher as a dwarf, compact plant of somewhat irregular shape that grew almost as broad as it was high. The growth rate was described as being less than 1" (2 cm) per year. The oldest known plant was estimated to be more than fifty years old and produced cones and fertile seeds. It was less than 2' (60 cm) tall. According to Teuscher, this selection also bred true from seed.

Teusher's description is for a plant found by Daniel M. St. George of Charlotte, Vermont, who collected *Tsuga canadensis* seedlings growing in the wild and sold them to various people. Between 1927 and 1934 St. George had found twenty-five similar, miniature plants growing on a ridge in the Green Mountains. He sold these to his special customers. Eventually he found the cone-bearing parent, which was over fifty years old and about 2' (60 cm) tall. It was an exceptionally dense, little plant.

In 1934, George Ehrle, a nurseryman from Clifton, New Jersey, purchased two of the remaining small plants from St. George for $5.00 each. Ehrle chopped up one plant for scion material, and the other was pictured and described as var. minuta by Henry Teuscher in "New Flora and Silva". When describing var. minuta, Teuscher used the parent plant found by St. George for much of his information.

Accounts of the origin of 'Minuta' are badly jumbled in the literature due to the confusion that has arisen between 'Minuta' and 'Abbott's Pygmy'. They are somewhat similar in appearance, but not identical either in characteristics or origin. They differ in growth rate and the size, shape and color of the leaves.

Tsuga canadensis 'Abbott's Pygmy' develops into an irregular globe with shorter leaves and less annual growth than 'Minuta'. Its leaves are small and pointed. They are dense and irregularly located along the tiny branches. The foliage is mid to light green while the buds are relatively large and easy to see.

(continued)

'Minuta'
Hillier Arboretum

'Abbott's Pygmy'
Coenosium Gardens

Tsuga canadensis 'Minuta' and its "Friends"
(cont.)

Tsuga canadensis 'Abbott's Pygmy' is very easy to confuse with *Tsuga canadensis* 'Minuta'. In fact, in the early literature the confusion was rather extensive. These two plants are very much alike and can only be distinguished by an expert. For the average person, either one will serve the same purpose in the landscape.

Collected by Frank L. Abbott in May, 1933, 'Abbott's Pygmy' was found north of Richmond, Chittenden County, Vermont, on the west side of the Winooski River. Since it was found on the same ridge as 'Minuta' (although some distance away) the two may be from the same seed parent.

Tsuga canadensis 'Little Joe', a third miniature, is a tight, congested bun. Its leaves are smaller than those of 'Minuta' and a darker green color. It can easily be confused with 'Minuta' and even 'Abbot's Pygmy', but it does form a more symmetrical globose shape than either of those cultivars. Its growth rate is slightly less than that of the other two. It was introduced by Mitsch Nursery in Aurora, Oregon, about 1987. The original seedling was sent to the nursery by Joseph Cessarini, then of Long Island, New York.

Tsuga canadensis 'Minuta' and its "friends" can serve the same role in the landscape. They will thrive in moderate shade but may burn in the full summer sun. These plants are exceptional selections for a rock garden. They need good drainage and should be sited in a shady location or on an eastern slope for the best results.

Top is 'Little Joe' and to the left is 'Minuta' in a planter, both at Coenosium Gardens

Tsuga canadensis 'Stewart's Gem'

The cultivars of *Tsuga canadensis* have been categorized into a number of neat little groups, two of which are "twiggy" and "cinnamon-tipped". These names are very desciptive of the plants. These groups were first set up by John Swartley in his Master's Thesis at Cornell University in the 1930's. The "cinnamon-tipped" group includes a number of very interesting selections, all of which share the characteristic of having each branch's or branchlet's terminal bud covered with a brown, fuzzy sheath.

One of the best members of the cinnamon-tipped hemlocks is *Tsuga canadensis* 'Stewart's Gem', discovered by Robert Stewart of Stewart's Nursery, Wakefield, Rhode Island, in 1936. He found it growing in the wild at Quinebaugh, Connecticut. Commonly grown from cuttings, it becomes wider than high, attaining a height of 15" (35 cm) with a width less than 3' (1 m) at thirty years. Sometimes this selection can be found under the name 'Rhode Island'.

All of the branches appear to radiate out from the center of the plant resulting in a slight depression at the center. It is very dense, and the cinnamon-tipped branches add considerable interest to its appearance. This plant can be best grown in well drained soil with partial to mostly shade. It will also tolerate full sun but, as with most hemlocks, should not be taken from a shady location into the full sun without some adaptation time or sun scalding can result.

Helms garden

An old specimen in the Harper garden

Tsuga canadensis 'Verkade Recurved'

When I first came across a small plant of *Tsuga canadensis* 'Verkade Recurved', I couldn't believe what I was seeing. I had been collecting conifers for several years and had seen a number of very unusual plants. This plant had curly needles and when I touched one of the branches, it broke off in my hand. It was so unique that I had to find one for my own garden. The plant I was looking at was growing in Layne Ziegenfuss' Hillside Gardens Nursery.

Behind his home Ziegenfuss had a polyhouse dug into a hillside. The poly hadn't been replaced for ten years, and the plants were growing in rusty, old fruit cans. The 'Verkade Recurved' was one of the "treasures" in a fruit can. Eventually I was able to talk Ziegenfuss out of the plant, and it became part of my garden.

Hillside Gardens Nursery was in decline when I met Ziegenfuss. Hundreds of treasures were scattered throughout the nursery, from the small plants in fruit cans to specimen stock plants scattered throughout the once manicured stock and landscape areas. Ziegenfuss knew everyone who was involved with conifers throughout the Northeast and had scaled Hillside Gardens Nursery back to strictly a grafted liner production operation. I used to sit for hours with him talking about conifers, people, and conifer grafting techniques. Eventually he was forced to quit grafting when he developed a latex allergy and could not work with rubber grafting bands.

'Verkade Recurved' is an open-growing, pyramidal plant with a very irregular growth habit. It has an annual growth of approximately 3" (7 cm) per year. The foliage is dark green with strikingly recurved needles, and the branches are so brittle that just touching them will sometimes break them from the plant. It was discovered by a hemlock collector who gave it to John Verkade, Verkade's Nursery, Wayne, New Jersey, who then introduced it into the nursery trade.

Tsuga canadensis 'Curly' is an upright, compact bush with leaves identical to 'Verkade Recurved'. It grows about 4" (10 cm) per year with dark green, strongly recurved needles. The branches and branchlets are brittle and will also break off at the slightest touch. Harold Epstein, Larchmont, New York, found the original plant in a friend's garden in 1969. It can easily be mistaken for *Tsuga canadensis* 'Verkade's Recurved', but *Tsuga canadensis* 'Curly' grows at a much faster rate.

'Verkade Recurved'
Coenosium Gardens

Tsuga mertensiana 'Elizabeth'

The Cascade Mountains of the Pacific Northwest are home to an exceptional alpine hemlock, *Tsuga mertensiana*. Twisted and gnarled forms of this hemlock are common near the snowline on the volcanic mountain peaks throughout the Cascades. Few *mertensiana* cultivars have been collected and grown. When dwarf plants are dug and planted at lower elevations, they either suffer from the change in growing conditions or adapt and show an accelerated growth rate.

However, there is one exceptional cultivar of this species that rivals any cultivar of the other hemlock species. Collected in 1940 on Mount Rainier, near Tacoma, Washington, by Elizabeth Frye, *Tsuga mertensiana* 'Elizabeth' is a spreading plant that grows twice as wide as high. The foliage is gray-blue, and its growth rate is about 3" (8 cm) per year. A typical plant is very dense with many branchlets forming along each of the side branches. It is propagated from cuttings with moderate success, which is the best way to maintain its character.

In 1971 James Caperci of Rainier Mountain Nursery in Seattle, Washington, had the original plant in his garden. It was 2' (60 cm) high by 4' (1.3 m) wide. He introduced it as *Tsuga mertensiana* 'Elizabeth', and it has proven to be reliable at lower elevations in the Northwest. I have found the growth rate will often exceed the published rate of 3" (8 cm) per year, but not by an amount to disqualify it as being suitable for the smaller garden.

Since it is of alpine origin, 'Elizabeth' is an excellent choice for a rock garden. Its spreading growth habit keeps its outline low without taking on a cushion shape, especially since the center is somewhat depressed and the main branches arch outward much like a fountain. Plant it in the full sun or partial shade in well drained soil.

Coenosium Gardens

Mitsch Nursery (left) and Coenosium Gardens with Tsuga mertensiana *'Blue Star' (above)*

Picture Information

The pictures in this book were taken by the author on trips throughout the United States and overseas. This list is a representation of the various places visited. More information on the public gardens may be found through a search of the internet.

Public Gardens

Arnold Arboretum- Jamaica Plain, MA
Bernheim Forest- Kentucky
Blijdenstein Pinetum - Holland
Boskoop Research Station- Holland
Coenosium Rock Garden- South Seattle Community College- Seattle, WA
Gimborn Pinetum- Holland
Hillier Arboretum- England
Masonic Home- Elizabethtown, PA
Pruhonice Arboretum- Czech Republic
Pruhonice Botanic Garden- Czech Republic
Heartland Collection- Bickelhaupt Arboretum, Iowa
RHS Garden Wisley- England
Saville Garden- England
Trompenburg Arboretum- Holland
Valley Garden- Windsor Great Park, England

Picture Information

Private Gardens and Nurseries

Balatka- Jiri Balatka, Czech Republic
Beran- Jan Beran, Czech Republic
Bloom- Adrian Bloom, Foggy Bottom, England
Brooks- Martin Brooks, Pennsylvania
Buchholz- Talon Buchholz, Oregon
Dibben- Derek Dibben, England
Esteldorfer- Franz Esteldorfer, Austria
Geers- Herman Geers, Holland
Halada- Milan Halada, Czech Republic
Hachman Nursery- Germany
Harper- Chub Harper, Illinois
Helms- David Helms, Washington
Horstmann- Gunter/Uwe Horstmann, Germany
Iseli Nursery- Oregon
Koelwyn- Leo Koelwyn, Australia
Koeman- Kas Koeman, Holland
Kohout- Jorg Kohout, Germany
Kools- Nelis Kools, Holland
Krejci- Ladislav Krejci, Czech Republic
Linssen- Wiel Linssen, Holland
Maly- Karel Maly, Czech Republic
Mitsch Nursery- Oregon
Reis- Joe Reis, New York
Ruis Nursery- Hungary
Stanley & Sons Nursery- Oregon
Sturm- Fremont Sturm, Oregon
Van Kempen- Hank Van Kempen, Holland
Vermeulen- Ronald Vermeulen, Holland

Index

Abies concolor 'Archer's Dwarf'	32
Abies concolor 'Piggelmee'	34
Abies koreana 'Blauer Eskimo'	36
Abies koreana 'Gait'	38
Abies koreana 'Kohout's Icebreaker'	40
Abies koreana 'Silberkugel'	42
Abies koreana 'Silberperle'	44
Abies lasiocarpa 'Alpine Beauty'	46
Abies lasiocarpa 'DuFlon'	48
Abies lasiocarpa 'Lopalpun'	50
Abies nord. 'Golden Spreader'	52
Abies procera 'Blaue Hexe'	54
Abies veitchii 'Heddergott'	56
Abies veitchii 'Heine'	56
Abies veitchii 'Rumburk'	56
Cedrus atlantica 'Lilliput'	58
Cedrus atl. 'Mt. Saint Catherine'	60
Cedrus brevifolia 'Kenwith'	62
Cedrus deodara 'Deep Cove'	64
Cedrus deodara 'Hollandia'	70
Cedrus deodara 'Limeglow'	68
Cedrus deodara 'Mountain Beauty'	68
Cedrus deodara 'Mylor'	68
Cedrus deodara 'Pygmy'	70
Cedrus deodara 'Scott'	68
Cedrus deodara 'Silver Mist'	64
Cedrus deodara 'Snow Sprite'	66
Cedrus deodara 'White Imp'	66
Cedrus libani 'Comte de Dijon'	72
Cedrus libani 'Green Prince'	74
Cedrus libani 'Nana'	72
Cedrus libani 'Sargentii'	76
Cedrus libani 'Taurus'	72
Cham. obtusa 'Bess'	78
Cham. obtusa 'Butterball'	82
Cham. obtusa 'Caespitosa'	86
Cham. obtusa 'Elf'	84
Cham. obtusa 'Golden Sprite'	82, 84
Cham. obtusa 'Hage'	94
Cham. obtusa 'JR'	88
Cham. obtusa 'Juniperoides'	86
Cham. obtusa 'Mariesii'	90
Cham. obtusa 'Nana'	92
Cham. obtusa 'Nana Lutea'	98
Cham. obtusa 'Nana Gracilis'	96
Cham. obtusa 'Snowkist'	100
Cham. obtusa 'Sparkles'	104
Cham. obtusa 'Spiralis'	78, 86
Cham. obtusa 'Verdon'	86, 98
Cham. pisifera 'Compacta'	106
Cham. pisifera 'Gold Dust'	106
Cham. pisifera 'Nana'	106
Cham. pisifera 'Silver Lode'	106
Crypt. japonica 'Kilmacurragh'	106
Crypt. japonica 'Knaptonesis'	110
Crypt. japonica 'Ryoku Gyoku'	112
Crypt. japonica 'Tansu'	114
Crypt. japonica 'Tenzan'	114
Picea abies 'Brno'	116
Picea abies 'Clanbrassiliana'	118
Picea abies 'Dumpy'	120
Picea abies 'Ellwangeriana'	122
Picea abies 'Formanek'	124
Picea abies 'Frohburg'	124
Picea abies 'Hildburghausen'	126
Picea abies 'Humilis'	128
Picea abies 'Little Gem'	130
Picea abies 'Malena'	132
Picea abies 'Nidiformis'	134
Picea abies 'Pachyphylla'	136
Picea abies 'Pumila Nigra'	138
Picea abies 'Pusch'	140
Picea abies 'Tabuliformis'	134
Picea abies 'Tufty'	142
Picea abies 'Wichtel'	128
Picea abies 'Witches' Brood'	144
Picea abies 'Zajecice'	146
Picea glauca 'Burning Well'	148
Picea glauca 'Palecek'	148
Picea glauca 'Cecilia'	150
Picea glauca 'Conica'	152
Picea glauca 'Daisey's White'	154

Index

Picea glauca 'Pixie'	154
Picea glauca 'Pixie Dust'	154
Picea glauca 'Rainbow's End'	154
Picea glauca 'Spring Surprise'	154
Picea omorika 'Elisabeth'	156
Picea omorika 'Gunter'	156
Picea omorika 'Nana'	158, 181
Picea omorika 'Peve Tijn'	158
Picea omorika 'Pimoko'	156
Picea omorika 'Treblitzsch'	160
Picea orient. 'Mt. Vernon'	162
Picea orient. 'Professor Langner'	164
Picea orient. 'Tom Thumb Gold'	166
Picea pungens 'Blue Pearl'	168
Picea pung. 'Donna's Rainbow'	170
Picea pungens 'Early Cones'	172
Picea pungens 'Frieda'	174
Picea pungens 'Hermann Naue'	172
Picea pungens 'Jean Iseli'	174
Picea pungens 'Pali'	176
Picea pungens 'Porcupine'	178
Picea pung. 'R. H. Montgomery'	180
Picea pungens 'St. Mary'	182
Picea pungens 'Yvette'	178
Picea smithiana 'Ballarat'	184
Pinus banksiana 'Chippewa'	186
Pinus banksiana 'Manomet'	187
Pinus cembra 'Aurea'	188
Pinus mugo 'Carstens'	192
Pinus mugo 'Fructata'	194
Pinus mugo 'Hvozdany'	196
Pinus mugo 'Jakobsen'	198
Pinus mugo 'Little Delight'	200
Pinus mugo 'Michelle'	204
Pinus mugo 'Nerost'	200
Pinus m. 'Sherwood Compact'	204
Pinus mugo 'Sleitzsky Dom'	200
Pinus mugo 'Zundert'	192
Pinus nigra 'Black Prince'	206
Pinus nigra 'Gaelle Bregeon'	210
Pinus nigra 'Helga'	206
Pinus nigra 'Oriesok'	206
Pinus nigra 'Pichounet'	208
Pinus nigra 'Pierrick Bregeon'	210
Pinus nigra 'Pipouniou'	208
Pinus parv. 'Adcock's Dwarf'	220
Pinus parv. 'Burke's Bonsai'	212
Pinus parv. 'Glauca Nana'	214
Pinus parv. 'Hagoromo'	216
Pinus parv. 'Kobe'	218
Pinus parv. 'Pygmy Yatsubusa'	220
Pinus parv. 'Regenhold'	226
Pinus parv. 'Tani-mano-yuki'	224
Pinus parv. 'Tsai's Cushion'	226
Pinus strobiformis 'Loma Linda'	228
Pinus strobus 'Greg'	230
Pinus strobus 'Horsford'	230
Pinus strobus 'Merrimack'	232
Pinus strobus 'Mini Twists'	234
Pinus strobus 'Sarah Rachel'	236
Pinus strobus 'Sea Urchin'	238
Pinus strobus 'Tiny Kurls'	234
Pinus strobus 'Uncatena'	230, 232
Pinus sylv. 'Bennett Compact'	240
Pinus sylv. 'Calle'	246
Pinus sylv. 'Cerik'	246
Pinus sylv. 'Globosa Viridis'	244
Pinus sylv. 'Hexguld'	246
Pinus sylv. 'Jeremy'	242
Pinus sylv. 'Little Ann'	242
Pinus sylv. 'Moseri'	244
Pinus sylv. 'Pixie'	242
Pinus thunbergiana 'Ogi'	248
Pinus uncinata 'Babay'	252
Pinus uncinata 'Eva'	252
Pinus uncinata 'Jesek'	252
Pinus uncinata 'Paradekissen'	250
Pseudotsuga menziesii 'Little Jon'	254
Taxus baccata 'Adpressa Aurea'	258
Taxus baccata 'Fastigiata Micro'	256

Index

Taxus baccata 'Fowle' — *258*
Taxus baccata 'Goldener Zwerg' — *256*
Taxus baccata 'Green Diamond' — *260*
Thuja occidentalis 'Mini Spiral' — *262*
Thuja occidentalis 'Miky' — *262*
Ts. can. 'Abbott's Pygmy' — *278*
Ts. can. 'Bacon Cristate' — *264*
Ts. can. 'Betty Rose' — *266*
Ts. can. 'Cole' — *268*
Ts. can. 'Curly' — *282*
Ts. can. 'Everitt Golden' — *270*
Ts. can. 'Horsford Contorted' — *272*
Ts. can. 'Jacqueline Verkade' — *274*
Ts. can. 'Jervis' — *276*
Ts. can. 'Little Joe' — *280*
Ts. can. 'Minuta' — *278*
Ts. can. 'Stewart's Gem' — *282*
Ts. can. 'Verkade Recurved' — *284*
Ts. het. 'Thorson's Weeping' — *268*
Ts. mertens. 'Elizabeth' — *286*